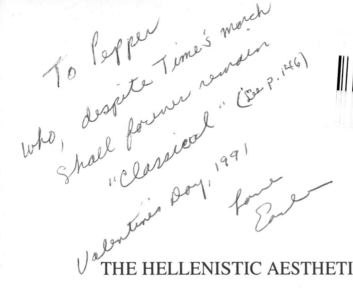

D0439378

THE HELLENISTIC AESTHETIC

THE
HELLENISTIC
AESTHETIC

———

Barbara Hughes Fowler

The University of Wisconsin Press

The University of Wisconsin Press
114 North Murray Street
Madison, Wisconsin 53715

Copyright © 1989
The Board of Regents of the University of Wisconsin System
All rights reserved

5   4   3   2   1

Printed in the United States of America

Library of Congress Cataloging-in-Publication Data
Fowler, Barbara Hughes, 1926–
The Hellenistic aesthetic/Barbara Hughes Fowler.
236 pp.   cm.—(Wisconsin studies in classics)
Bibliography: pp. 207–210
Includes index.
1. Greek poetry, Hellenistic—History and criticism.   2. Art and
literature—Greece.   3. Aesthetics, Ancient.   4. Art, Hellenistic.
5. Hellenism.   I. Title.   II. Series.
PA3081.F6   1989
881'.0109—dc20   88-40433
ISBN 0-299-12040-6   CIP
ISBN 0-299-12044-9 (pbk.)

to the memory of
Richmond Lattimore

But such a form as Grecian goldsmiths make . . .

Contents

Illustrations

Preface

I am well aware of the hazards of attempting a work, however modest in scale or scope, upon the Hellenistic aesthetic. Almost all dates for both poems and works of art in this period are insecure. In addition, we must rely for the art in large part upon Roman copies, which may or may not be entirely faithful to the originals. I do, however, believe that the Hellenistic age was more or less of a piece, that themes, subject matter, and even styles, despite their very great variety, persisted in fair degree throughout the last three centuries B.C. I have accepted only the conventional and most general kind of dating, and I have been careful not to give the impression that poems and works of art were contemporary when in fact they probably were not. In no case have I tried to date one art form by another. I have tried merely to show that the various art forms shared in a common aesthetic and, by this means, to introduce students to the delights of the Hellenistic period. My notes and bibliography will lead the curious to works that are both more general and more detailed.

This book is primarily about the poetry of the Hellenistic period. Then it is about certain of the visual arts: sculpture, painting, mosaics, and jewelry. I have done little with architecture and nothing at all with military monuments. I have not discussed philosophical or rhetorical schools, nor have I dealt with drama. I have not used the fragments in the *Supplementum Hellenisticum* of Parsons and Lloyd-Jones or in Powell's *Collecteana Alexandrina*, because I thought them too lacking in context to be of interest to my audience. I realize that all these contributed to the Hellenistic aesthetic, but I hope that I shall be forgiven for limiting my inquiry to those facets of the culture that I understand best.

I use the term "Hellenistic" to refer to the period of time between the death of Alexander in 323 B.C. and the death of Augustus in 14 A.D. I use the term "Alexandrian" to refer either to those works which we know to have originated in the city of Alexandria or to the aesthetic qualities which are commonly associated with them: prettiness, playfulness, and a lightness of tone.

All translations from the Greek, unless otherwise noted, are my own.

I should like to thank former Chancellor Irving Shain and the University of Wisconsin Foundation for the award and funding of my Bascom Professorship which allowed me to visit museums in Europe and North Africa and contributed in other ways also to the preparation of this book; my research assistants Lucinda Alwa and Jeffrey Pinkham; Paul Plass and Martin Winkler, who read the manuscript and made valuable suggestions; Norma Maynard, who typed and helped edit the manuscript; Lloyd Holm and Joy DeStefano, who gave special kinds of encouragement; Barbara Hanrahan, Carol Olsen, and Elizabeth Steinberg of the University of Wisconsin Press for their gracious support; and above all my colleague and friend Warren Moon, who supplied both bibliography and inspiration.

Abbreviations Used in Notes

I have used the following abbreviations in the notes:

Bieber   M. Bieber, *The Sculpture of the Hellenistic Age* (New York, 1961)

Charbonneaux J. Charbonneaux, R. Martin, and F. Villard, *Hellenistic Art, 330–50 B.C.* (London, 1973)

Havelock, *HA*   C. M. Havelock, *Hellenistic Art* (Greenwich, Conn., 1971; 2nd ed., New York, 1981)

Onians   J. Onians, *Art and Thought in the Hellenistic Age* (London 1979)

Pollitt, *AHA*   J. J. Pollitt, *Art in the Hellenistic Age* (Cambridge, 1986)

RE   Pauly-Wissowa, *Real-Enzyclopädie der klassichen Altertumwissenschaft*

THE HELLENISTIC AESTHETIC

Introduction

Critics have said of Hellenistic poetry that it is decadent, learned, and jejune.[1] These are charges that can be leveled at the worst of it: some of the epigrams in the *Anthology*, parts of Callimachus, and all of Lycophron. Yet one can say of much of it that it is witty, elegant, and technically refined. It may lack the matutinal freshness of the archaic lyricists, the orphic splendor of Pindar, the high passion of the fifth-century tragedians, but it must in its own day have been important, have appealed to and shaped the taste of its time. Certainly it changed the course of Western literature. It initiated the pastoral, reworked the epic tradition. It inspired the Augustan poets and the twentieth-century Alexandrian Cavafy, and its spirit is to some degree alive still in Lawrence Durrell's *Alexandria Quartet*. It may lack the resonance that the Roman poets brought to it from their own Italian setting or the simple passion with which Cavafy imbued it from his personal, erotic experience. Nevertheless, it has a sparkle and music of its own and ought certainly to be appreciated for what it in its own right is.

1. For instance, C. A. Trypanis, "The Character of Alexandrian Poetry," *Greece and Rome* 16 (1947) 6–7: "But no matter how science flourishes, the decline of literature and poetry is a sure index of moral decay. . . . How else could the great fountain of inspiration, joy and sorrow, remain silent without finding their singers? . . . Their soul seems to have been parched by their endless studies and annotations; their imaginations and their feelings became arid and sterile." Cf. A. Körte, *Hellenistic Poetry*, trans. J. Hammer and M. Hadas (New York, 1929) 9, who takes a somewhat more positive view: "The heavy demands the poets have made upon the knowledge, nay, often upon the erudition of their audience and readers, plainly enhances with the initiated the charm of their works. Compared with the lusty virgin growth of classical poetry, the Hellenistic is for the most part a domesticated or even a hothouse plant; but its flowers, cultivated with conscious art, have, for all that, a beauty of color and a delicacy of fragrance which still possess the power to delight and charm."

Hellenistic poetry brought to Western literature many of the qualities which we think of as modern: an interest in animals (especially pets), babies, children, women, and grotesques; common or working people and the tools of their trades; landscapes; cities; the passions of romantic love and of sinning; pathos; burlesque. The literature parallels the subject matter of the visual arts, where we find fishermen, hunchbacks, dancing dwarfs, drunken old women, babies, dogs, women who have died in childbirth, kitchen utensils, and the expression of emotion in the faces of creatures as well as people.

The new interest in genre scenes, in everyday people and their pursuits, is commonly understood to be the result of the decline of the city-state. Just as people, deprived of a common moral purpose, turned to the individualistic philosophies of Stoicism and Epicureanism, so artists turned to the portrayal of the personal passions, the particulars of life. Literature became romantic rather than classical. So much surely is true. There were, however, other factors that shaped the literary and visual arts of the period. What went hand in hand with an interest in the particular and the individual was an increasing realism. That realism was a product of an increase in technical proficiency, which was in itself a result in part of the new science. The Hellenistic poets and artists were especially interested in technique. This appears not only in their subject matter itself but also in the craft which presented that subject matter. The two are quite inseparable. It is this interaction of poet and artist, of subject and craft, that I wish to explore.[2]

2. I do not intend to make the specific sort of comparisons that T. B. L. Webster, *Hellenistic Poetry and Art* (London, 1964), or S. Nicosia, *Teocrito e l'arte figurata* (Palermo, 1968), do, but rather to look for common aesthetic principles: mood, theme, and technique.

I

Craft and Elegance

Craft is a mark of Hellenistic poetry and art. In poetry this appears in metrical refinement;[1] in art, in technical virtuosity. In the poetry there are, apart from its musicality,[2] reflections of the technical virtuosity of the visual arts. Although one cannot truly separate these from other aspects of the Hellenistic aesthetic, such as magic, eroticism, and a sense of the sweetness of nature, one can for the purposes of analysis look at certain of them in relative isolation.

In Theocritus' *Idyll* I, the description of the cup which the goatherd offers to Thyrsis as a gift in return for his song exemplifies a number of themes and techniques of the Hellenistic aesthetic.[3] Inside the cup a woman has been fashioned (τέτυκται 32). She is such a thing as gods might work (δαίδαλμα

1. See esp. A. W. Bulloch, "A Callimachean Refinement to the Greek Hexameter," *Classical Quarterly* 20 (1970) 258–68. On technique in general see also G. Capovilla, "Nuovi contributi a Callimaco," *Studi Italiani di Filologia Classica* 42 (1970) 94–153; D. A. Kidd, "The Fame of Aratus," *AUMLA* no. 15 (1961) 5–18; V. Citti, "Lettura di Arato," *Vichiana* 2 (1965) 146–70; J. Ferguson, "The Epigrams of Callimachus," *Greece and Rome* 17 (1970) 64–80; L. H. Gold, "Adjectives in Theocritus: A Study of Poetic Diction in the Pastoral Idylls" (diss. Univ. of Wisconsin, Madison, 1976); G. Giangrande, *Zu Sprachgebrauch, Technik und Text des Apollonius Rhodios, Class. and Byz. Monogr.* I (Amsterdam, 1973); D. M. Halperin, *Before Pastoral: Theocritus and the Ancient Tradition of Bucolic Poetry* (New Haven, 1983) app. "Bucolic Diaeresis and Bucolic Genre," 259–66.

2. On musicality in the Hellenistic poets see especially J. K. Newman, *The Classical Epic Tradition* (Madison, 1986) 21, 100–102, but also K. J. McKay, *The Poet at Play: Kallimachos, The Bath of Pallas*, Supp. VI to *Mnemosyne* (Leiden, 1962) 82–90.

3. For recent treatments of the ivy cup, its decoration, and its relevance to the poem as a whole, see S. F. Walker, *Theocritus* (Boston, 1980) 36–37, and Halperin, *Before Pastoral*, ch. 9, "Three Scenes on an Ivy-Cup." Halperin gives a bibliography to date on p. 161, n. 50.

5

1. Achilles surrendering Briseis, Museo Nazionale, Naples

32). She is bedecked (ἀσκητά 33) with cloak and diadem. The Greek words all imply technique. Two men contend, alternately (ἀμοιβαδίς 34), for her in words, but this does not touch her heart; first she smiles at one, then casts (ῥιπτεῖ 37) her mind to the other. Gow remarks that ῥιπτεῖ "casts" is heightened from τρέπει "turns".[4] Of ἀμοιβαδίς "alternately" he says, "For the next three lines, more than anywhere else in his account of the bowl, T. is interpreting rather than describing, since a work of art can only suggest, not

4. A.S.F. Gow, _Theocritus_ II (Cambridge, 1965) 9 on line 37.

2. Smiling child, British Museum, London

3. Smiling little girl, Palazzo Grazioli, Rome

depict, successive action on the part of the figures."[5] This is, of course, true, but the achievement of Hellenistic sculpture and painting was to heighten suggestion; to make obvious a casting of the mind, a give-and-take of conversation. In the Pompeian wall painting showing Achilles' surrender of Briseis, there can be no doubt that Achilles is casting his thought as well as his glance toward Briseis (fig. 1). He is, among other things, angry. Another achievement was the naturalistic, not the archaic, smile.[6] An especially enchanting example is that of a child in the British Museum (fig. 2); another, that on the bronze statuette of a little girl in the Palazzo Grazioli in Rome (fig. 3).

5. Ibid. on line 34.
6. G.M.A. Hanfmann, "Hellenistic Art," *Dumbarton Oaks Papers* 17 (1963) 85.

4. Demosthenes, Ny Carlsberg Glyptotek, Copenhagen

On the cup the men, long hollow-eyed from love (ὑπ' ἔρωτος δηθὰ κυλοιδιόωντες 37–38), labor in vain. Eros, personified or not, is a powerful force in Hellenistic poetry and art, and here his effect is realistic. The suitors are really puffy-eyed; they have, as our idiom goes, "bags under their eyes." The word κυλοιδιάω "hollow-eyed" is used in Aristophanes (*Lys.* 472) of the results of a blow and in Nicander as the effect of poison (*Al.* 478). Heliodorus (IV.7.7) uses it of a lover. The men suffer presumably from insomnia. Detail of this sort is common in portrait sculpture of the period. A particularly good example is the statue of Demosthenes, a Roman copy of a third-century original, in the Ny Carlsburg Glyptotek, Copenhagen, where the thin body continues to express the ascetic, even neurasthenic anguish of the lean, pinched face with its hollowed cheeks and deeply furrowed brow. Here is a man worn out, embittered by his passion (fig. 4).

Next to the woman and her suitors there is fashioned (τέτυκται 39) inside the cup an old fisherman and a rugged rock. Rough-rocked landscapes appear in relief sculpture at about this time, and fishermen are common subjects in both poetry and art. *Idyll* XXI—attributed, probably wrongly, [7] to Theocritus —gives a detailed and realistic picture of two poor fishermen in their cottage amid the implements of their craft: "baskets and rods, hooks and weedy baits, lines and reels and pots of woven rush, cords and oars and aged skiff upon its props, a bit of matting beneath the head, their clothes, their caps" (trans. Gow).[8] The theme of the poor fisherman, as Gow reminds us, goes back at least to Menander, who wrote a Ἁλιεῖς,[9] and appears frequently in Book VII of the *Anthology*. Leonidas (XX; *AP* 7.295) especially gives us a realistic picture of a fisherman, Theris, who rode the sea more than a gull and was a preyer on fishes, a hauler of nets, a prober of clefts; he died not in a storm but in his own reed hut, quenched like a lamp by the length of his years. His tomb was set up not by his children or wife but by the guild of his fellow fishermen.

The fisherman in *Idyll* I is eagerly gathering up a large net for a cast; he is like (ἐοικώς 41) a man laboring mightily. Realism is the point here. You would say (φαίης κεν 42) that he was fishing with all the strength of his limbs—so do the sinews swell (ᾠδήκαντι . . . ἶνες 43) all about his neck, old though he is. The verb "swell" here is especially plastic, and the potential optative "you would say" emphasizes too the realism of the carving. There are many such sinewy fishermen, often old, in Hellenistic sculpture, and sometimes details of landscape, like the rugged rock here, are suggested or shown. Some of the fishermen too have with them the implements of their craft. The fisherman in the British Museum stands on a rough surface, which may be rock or sand, and has in one hand a basket which is set upon some detail of landscape, perhaps a tree trunk. His scanty exomis reveals a body which is muscular and sinewy in the extreme (fig. 5). A black marble statue in the Louvre of an old, partly bald, unevenly bearded fisherman, who appears to stand knee-deep in water, should, Bieber asserts, be "reconstructed with a pail in the left hand for his catch, and the fishing rod in his right hand." [10] This statue is remarkable for its realism. The wasted muscles and dilated veins are meticulously portrayed, and the upraised eyes contribute to an expression which may be read as either ethereal or stupid (fig. 6).[11]

7. Gow, *Theocritus* II, 369–70.
8. Ibid. I, 153.
9. Ibid. II, 369.
10. Bieber 142.
11. Ibid. 142 and fig. 595; H. P. Laubscher, *Fischer und Landleute: Studien zur Hellenistischen Genreplastik* (Mainz am Rhein, 1982) 49–58; Pollitt, *AHA* 143 and fig. 155. On the type of the fisherman in Hellenistic sculpture see also E. Bayer, *Fischerbilder in der Hellenistischen Plastik* (Bonn, 1983). Cf. N. Himmelmann, *Alexandria und der Realismus in der griechischen Kunst* (Tübingen, 1983) 26–27.

5. Fisherman, British Museum,
London

The third scene carved within the cup is that of a small boy plaiting a locust cage, while two foxes go up and down. One fox is plundering the vine rows; the other is bringing her wit to bear upon the boy's wallet. Children and animals are common subject matter in Hellenistic art. There are a number of statues of children with pets: a boy with a deer and a girl with a hare, both in the Louvre (figs. 7 and 8); a terra cotta at the Walters Art Gallery in Baltimore of two little boys watching a cockfight (fig. 9); and the well-known toddler in the Glyptothek in Munich and in the Museo Capitolino in Rome strangling his pet goose (fig. 10). Here again, in Theocritus' *Idyll*, vocabulary suggests craft. One fox goes to and fro (φοιτῇ 49); only technique can suggest such movement. The other brings all her wit (πάντα δόλον τεύχοισα 50) to bear upon raiding the boy's breakfast bread. The vocabulary denotes an abstract concept but connotes technique. Τεύχω has been used above to refer concretely to fashioning. The child weaves (πλέκει 52) the pretty locust cage,

6. Fisherman, Louvre, Paris

fitting (ἐφαρμόσδων 53) stalks of asphodel with rush. We are told just how the cage is being made.

Lifelike carving distinguishes the scenes within the cup. The interest here is in technique.[12] Other features of the cup suggest nature and its sweetness in ways that are more sensuous, if less realistic. The cup is newly fashioned (νεοτευχές 28), perhaps of ivy wood—it is called κισσύβιον (27)[13]—washed over with sweet (ἁδέι 27) wax, and still fragrant (ποτόσδον 28) from the knife. Ivy winds (μαρύεται 29) above along its lips, ivy dusted with helichryse, and along that twists the tendril glowing with its yellow fruit (καρπῷ ἕλιξ είλεῖται ἀγαλλομένα κροκόεντι 31). Helichryse here may, as Gow suggests, refer only to the yellow fruit of the ivy. Theocritus would then be describing a common decorative pattern of his own day.[14] Since, however, helichryse was a plant with upright stems crowned by yellow flower clusters

12. Others have seen the scenes within the cup as primarily programmatic or even symbolic. See esp. C. Segal, "Since Daphnis Dies: The Meaning of Theocritus' First Idyll," reprinted from *Museum Helveticum* 31 (1974) 1–22 in *Poetry and Myth in Ancient Pastoral* (Princeton, 1981) 25–46. See also note 3, above.

13. See Gow, *Theocritus* II, 6 on line 27; Halperin, *Before Pastoral* 167–74.

14. Gow, *Theocritus* II, 7 on lines 20f.

7. Boy with deer, Louvre, Paris

and commonly used in garlands, there seems no reason not to take the phrase at face value.[15] This cup was special; it had a border of interwoven ivy and helichryse. It is the mention of color here that is both naturalistic and fanciful, for there is no reason to suppose that the cup was painted. The participle ἀγαλλομένα is especially vivid; the basic notion in the word is "light" or "glow."[16] Similarly, the vineyard below is described as weighted with dusky or reddening (περκναῖσι 46) clusters. The line is sensuous, naturalistic, and yet artificial. The color must be purely imaginary. There is here a sense of the sweetness of nature, and yet it is suggested purely by craft.

Throughout the description of the cup the sensuousness is underscored, as

15. But see K. J. Gutzwiller, "The Plant Decoration on Theocritus' Ivy Cup," *American Journal of Philology* 107 (1986) 253–55.

16. J. Pokorny, *Indogermanisches etymologisches Wörterbuch* I (Bern and Munich, 1959) 366.

8. Girl with hare, Louvre, Paris

it is everywhere in Theocritus, by sound patterns: alliteration particularly, but assonance too. Here Alexandrian musicality is a technique that enhances the description of technique. The cup is washed over with sweet wax, κισσύβιον κεκλυσμένον . . . κηρῷ: the three initial κ's, the internal σ's, and the assonance in υ give the line (27) a honey sweetness punctuated by soft palatal sounds. Line 30 is distinguished by alliteration: four κ's are quite evenly spaced:

κισσὸς ἑλιχρύσῳ κεκονιμένος· ἁ δὲ κατ' αὐτόν.

Line 31 is embraced by καρπῷ . . . κροκόεντι, and similarly sounding ἕλιξ εἱλεῖται come between. The sharp sounds beginning and ending the line are softened by ἀγαλλομένα, which is as sensuous in sound as it is in meaning. Line 39 is marked by an alliterative pattern: τ...τ...γ...τ...γ...τ...τ...τ...τ...τ:

τοῖς δὲ μετὰ γριπεύς τε γέρων πέτρα τε τέτυκται.

9. Boys watching cock fight, Walters Art Gallery, Baltimore

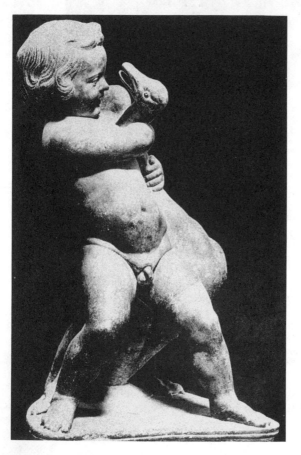

10. Toddler strangling goose, Museo Capitolino, Rome

14

Here key words—"fisherman," "old," and "fashioned"—are emphasized by the repeated consonants. In 41 again important words, "laboring" and "mightily," are marked by alliteration: κάμνοντι . . . καρτερόν.

In *Idyll* I the goatherd's cup is so wonderfully wrought that it suggests real people and animals engaged in actual human and animal pursuits. The workmanship suggests too the shapes and scents and colors of nature. Apollonius of Rhodes in the third book of the *Argonautica* describes workmanship of another, still more magical kind. Aphrodite promises Eros that if he will with one of his arrows kindle in Medea a passion for Jason, she will give him Zeus' very beautiful toy which his nurse Adrasteia had made for him when he was just a child. The ball is well-rounded (σφαῖραν εὐτρόχαλον 135). Its zones are fashioned of gold (χρύσεα μέν οἱ κύκλα τετεύχαται 137), and around each, double seams wind in a circle (ἀμφὶ δ' ἑκάστῳ / διπλόαι ἁψῖδες περιηγέες εἰλίσσονται 138). The stitches are hidden, and a dark blue spiral runs over them all (κρυπταὶ δὲ ῥαφαί εἰσιν, ἕλιξ δ' ἐπιδέδρομε πάσαις / κυανέη 139–40). There has been much debate about the exact appearance of this ball,[17] but what is of interest here is the vocabulary. Some of it occurred in the description of Theocritus' cup in *Idyll* I—forms of τεύχω (fashion) and words for spiral, ἕλιξ and εἰλίσσονται. Goldsmiths, in making Hellenistic jewelry, perhaps the most elegant art form of the period, twisted gold to make fine decorative wire. They also were wonderfully clever at concealing the joins in their work. And they used colored enamels to decorate their gold ornaments. Hoffman describes a late-fourth-century bracelet: "The 'collars' behind the lion-heads are of unusual length; they are profusely decorated with a floral motif executed in delicate spiral-spool and plain-wire filigree and inlaid with well preserved green and blue enamel." [18] There may be a suggestion of the goldworkers' craft in the description of Zeus' ball. That skill resulted in a ball that had magical properties, for when it was cast, like a star, it sent a trail of flame through the air (140–41).

Craft resulting in near magic occurs earlier in the *Argonautica* (1.721ff.) in the description of Jason's cloak.[19] It was a purple mantle of double fold (δίπλακα πορφυρέην 722), and Jason buckled (περονήσατο 722) it at the shoulder. It was the gift of Pallas Athene "when she first laid the keel-props of

17. For three very different reconstructions of this ball, none of which I find intelligible, see G. W. Mooney, *Apollonius Rhodius, Argonautica* (Dublin, 1912; repr. Amsterdam, 1964) 231 on lines 137ff.; M. M. Gillies, "The Ball of Eros," *Classical Review* 38 (1924) 50–51; O. Lendle, "Die Spiegelkugel des Zeus," *Hermes* 107 (1979) 493–95.

18. H. Hoffman and P. Davidson, *Greek Gold: Jewelry from the Age of Alexander* (Boston, Museum of Fine Arts; New York, Brooklyn Museum; Richmond, Virginia Museum of Fine Arts, 1966) 166–67 and figs. 60a and b.

19. On the thematic and symbolic significance of this cloak see G. Lawall, "Apollonius' *Argonautica*: Jason as Anti-Hero," *Yale Classical Studies* 19 (1966) 154–59; D. N. Levine, "Δίπλαξ πορφυρέη," *Rivista di Filologia e di Istruzione Classica* 98 (1970) 17–36; Newman, *The Classical Epic Tradition* 77–81.

11. Alexander Mosaic, Museo Nazionale, Naples

the Argo and taught Jason how to measure timbers with the rule" (723–24)—a gift of the goddess of craft when she taught the hero his craft. You could more easily cast your eyes upon the rising sun, for in the middle it was fashioned red (ἐρευθήεσσα τέτυκτο 727), but its borders were all of purple (πορφυρέη 728). Greek color terms, which seem to refer more to a play of light upon surfaces than to what we think of as hue, are never parallel to ours.[20] The colors of the cloak are apparently like those of the sunrise—rosy to scarlet. The word ἔρευθος "red" is thematic in the *Argonautica*;[21] it will take on several qualities and be a part not only of the magic but of the eroticism that pervades the poem. On each border many intricate designs (δαίδαλα 729) had been separately spread (ἐπέπαστο 729).[22] The first scene described is that of the Cyclopes hard at their work making a thunderbolt for Zeus. It was in its brightness almost fashioned (τόσον ἤδη παμφαίνων ἐτέτυκτο 731–32)—it lacked but one ray, which they were beating out with their hammers while it seethed with breath of ravening flame. Here are the world's finest craftsmen at work making brightness in the glare of their fiery forges. The light is also a part of the magic of the *Argonautica*.

One scene on the cloak in particular parallels the visual arts. "Long-haired Cytherea had been wrought (ἤσκητο) gripping the swift shield of Ares. From her shoulder to her left arm the fastening of her tunic was loosed beneath her breast, and opposite in her bronze shield her image appeared clear to see just as she stood" (742–46). The diagonal of her dress foretells or reflects the strong diagonals of Hellenistic art, and reflections in shields occur in both the Alexander Mosaic (fig. 11) and in the painting of Thetis in the workshop of Hephaestus (fig. 12). Both the visual arts and the *Argonautica* reflect the Hellenistic interest in optics.[23]

As Jason with his gorgeous cloak went to the city, he was "like a shining star which young girls who are kept in newly built chambers see rising above their houses; through the dark (κυανέοιο) air it charms their eyes as it glows beautifully red (καλὸν ἐρευθόμενος), and the maiden rejoices longing for the youth who is with strangers, for whom her parents are keeping her for his bride. Like that star the hero took his path to the city" (774–81). He himself has the red-gold glow of the cloak, of the star in the blue-black sky that makes the virgin girl think of her love.

In Book III of the *Argonautica*, when Aphrodite approached Eros, she found him playing with Ganymede at golden dice. He, the greedy child, had his hand quite full of them, and "a sweet blush (ἔρευθος) bloomed upon his cheeks" (121–22). The scene of the boys playing dice is thought to be a

20. See B. H. Fowler, "The Archaic Aesthetic," *American Journal of Philology* 105 (1984) 127–33.
21. See Newman, *The Classical Epic Tradition* 74–83.
22. Ruhnken's emendation. The manuscripts read ἐκέκαστο "had excelled."
23. See below, Chapters 9 and 12.

12. Thetis in workshop of Hephaestus, Museo Nazionale, Naples

description of a statue by Polycleitos mentioned in Pliny (*NH* XXXIV.55).[24] That statue has not survived, but we do have a third century B.C. terra-cotta of two young women playing at knucklebones (fig. 13). That the knucklebones are in Apollonius golden is a part of the magic. When later in Book III Eros shoots his arrow at Medea, the bolt burns like a flame. She casts bright glances at Jason, and "her soft cheeks change color, now to pale (ἐς χλόον), now to

24. See, for instance, Mooney, *Apollonius Rhodius* 229 on line 117.

13. Two young women playing at knucklebones, British Museum, London

red (ἔρευθος) in her mind's confusion" (297–98). Later, when Jason comes to Medea, "like the star Sirius coming from Ocean, which rises fair and clear to see but brings unspeakable disaster to flocks, . . . her heart falls from out of her breast, her eyes are misted over, and a hot blush (θερμὸν . . . ἔρευθος) spreads over her cheeks" (957–63).

The craft, the magic, the eroticism inherent in the word ἔρευθος "red", in the theme of gold and the concept of shining, come to fulfillment in Book IV of the *Argonautica* when Jason takes in his hands the golden fleece.[25] "As a maiden catches the gleam (αἴγλην) of the moon on her delicate robe as it rises above her high-roofed chamber, and her heart rejoices as she looks at its lovely ray (σέλας), so did Jason then delight as he lifted the great fleece in his hands, and on his fair (ξανθῇσι) cheeks and brow from the glittering (μαρμαρυγῇ) of the wool there settled a flush (ἔρευθος) like a flame (φλογὶ εἴκελον)" (167–73). Here surely is the chiaroscuro of the painters. Light and shade are as important as the colors themselves.

Finally, the Argonauts spread the wedding couch for Medea and Jason with the glittering golden fleece (χρύσεον αἰγλῆεν κῶας 1142). "The nymphs gathered for them flowers of varied color (ποικίλα) in their shining white

25. C. R. Beye, "Jason as Love-Hero in Apollonius' *Argonautica*," *Greek, Roman, and Byzantine Studies* 10 (1969) 31–55, sees the golden fleece as symbolic of Medea's virginity. I cannot myself believe that the ancients wrote with this kind of self-conscious symbolism.

14. Silver dish from Iran, Brooklyn
Museum, New York

bosoms (λευκοῖς . . . κόλποις), and a gleam as of fire (πυρὸς ὥς . . . αἴγλη) played over them all—such a light flashed from the golden tufts (τοῖον ἀπὸ χρυσέων θυσάνων ἀμαρύσσετο φέγγος)" (1143–46). Here the sweetness of nature mingles with the magic of the fleece and the love theme. The scene is coloristic too in the manner of the painters.

In the second century B.C. we have in Moschus' *Europa* another conspicuous example of a description of craftsmanship. The basket which Europa carried to gather flowers from the meadows was made of gold—a marvel, a wonder to behold, the work of Hephaestus. In it were fashioned many glittering and skillfully wrought things (δαίδαλα πολλὰ τετεύχατο μαρμαίροντα 43). This is familiar vocabulary. There was Io, fashioned of gold (χρυσοῖο τετυγμένη 44). She went to and fro (φοιταλέη 46), using her feet like (ἰκέλη 47) a swimmer—motion which though clumsily, or humorously, described can on the cup be shown only by the artisan's skill. The sea was fashioned of dark blue (κυάνου δ' ἐτέτυκτο 47). The Nile was made of silver, the heifer of bronze, and Zeus himself was fashioned of gold (χρυσοῦ . . . τετυγμένος 54). Beneath the rim of the rounded basket Hermes was wrought (ἤσκητο 56), and nearby Argos, who surpassed all others in unsleeping eyes, lay outstretched. "From his crimson (φοινήεντος) blood there rose a bird, glorying in the many-flowered hue of his plumage (ἀγαλλόμενος πτερύγων πολυανθέι χροιῇ), which he unfolded until like some swift-sailing ship he covered with his tail the lips of the golden basket" (58–59). This basket is imaginary and of course extraordinary, but Hellenistic silver work was often gilded, and polychrome inlays were a mark of Hellenistic gold work. The ecphrasis has a basis in reality.

A small silver dish in the Brooklyn Museum, reported to be from Iran and dated to the second half of the second century B.C., has a pattern of lotus petals and overlapping windblown acanthus leaves in double cruciform pattern (fig. 14). There are pairs of leaves and blossoms around the edge, and

15. Silver cosmetic box and lid, Antikenmuseum, West Berlin

small almond-shaped petals on the lotus and acanthus. There were probably semiprecious stones in the sockets of the four pairs of leaves, the blossoms, and the central flower. The dish and most of the exterior relief were cast, the details chased, and the reliefs gilded. A silver cosmetic box from Italy, now in the Staatliches Museum, West Berlin, dating to the second or first century B.C. is at least as elaborate as Europa's basket (fig. 15). The lid has a high-relief still life, featuring a cow's head with a tasseled rope garland around the horns. One horn serves as the handle of the box's lid. Around the calf's head are a ram's and a goat's head, a kid, a bird, a bunch of grapes, two loaves of bread, an ear of corn, a fig, other fruits and vegetables, and several unidentified objects. On one side of the box is a relief of what appears to be Leda and the swan. A nude woman with rather plump buttocks and thighs stands with her back turned to us. An equally plump, somewhat clumsy looking swan has in its mouth one end of a cloak which the woman is trying to throw over herself. A water jug, covered with another garment, stands at the foot of a column topped by a statue of Priapus. A tree with fairly elaborate foliage stands at the other side of the woman. The box is only 4½ inches (11.0 cm) high and 2⅞ inches (7.3 cm) wide. In contrast, Europa's basket does not seem a particularly ambitious piece of work. The actual and the literary works share too a certain clumsiness which may be deliberately humorous.

In the Hellenistic poets descriptions of elegant works of art are done with words denoting craft or technique, enhanced by such musical devices as alliteration and assonance, themselves a form of technique, and these descriptions reflect the techniques of the visual arts, such as filigree, enamelling, gilding, and chiaroscuro. Elegance and craft are in both the poets and the artists inextricably intertwined.

II

The Sweetness of Nature

Hellenistic poets described scenes from nature on works of art. They also described in their art nature itself. They were concerned, in descriptions both of its reproduction in works of art and its reality, with its sweetness. Some of this feeling seems to derive from the archaic lyricists and may be seen as a form of archaizing.[1] The Hellenistic poets, however, increased and enhanced it.

In Callimachus—the most artificial of the Alexandrians—we find, surprisingly, exceedingly delicate descriptions of nature. In the *Hymn to Apollo*, immediately following the ritual cry ἰὴ ἰὴ Καρνεῖε πολύλλιτε "Joy, joy, Carneius of many prayers," we have the lines:

> σεῖο δὲ βωμοί
> ἄνθεα μὲν φορέουσιν ἐν εἴαρι τόσσα περ ᾿Ωραι
> ποικίλ᾿ ἀγινεῦσι ζεφύρου πνείοντος ἐέρσην,
> χείματι δὲ κρόκον ἡδύν.
>
> (80–83)

Your altars wear flowers in spring—all the pied blossoms that the Hours bring forth when the west wind breathes dew, and in winter the sweet crocus.

Flowers were important to the archaic lyricists, in love songs and in drinking songs, and the adjectives ποικίλος "pied" and ἡδύς "sweet" were common in these early poets. In the Callimachean passage, in the genitive absolute, "the west wind breathing dew," we have, however, an advance in lyric feeling.

In the Callimachean *Hymn to Demeter* there is a description of the goddess's grove. In it were pine, great elms, pear and lovely sweet-apple trees

---

1. See below, Chapter 11.

(γλυκύμαλα 27–28). The particulars are in themselves appealing, and the sweet apples, reminiscent of Sappho, 105 (a) 1, enhance the description.[2] There follows an original Callimachean touch: "Water like amber rushed up from the ditches" (τὸ δ' ὥστ' ἀλέκτρινον ὕδωρ / ἐξ ἀμαρᾶν ἀνέθυε 28–29).

In the *Aitia* (II.43) Callimachus, again in a manner that recalls the archaic lyricists, mentions soft amber ointments with fragrant garlands (ξαν[θὰ σὺν εὐόδμοις ἀβρὰ λίπ]η στεφάνο[ις 13),[3] but then with a touch of his own says that they breathed no more (ἄπνο[α πάντ' ἐγένοντο 14).

A fragment of the *Hecale* describes the translucence of the sky at noon: "When, then, it was still midday, and the earth was warm, for so long was the glittering heaven more bright than glass (ὑάλοιο φαάντερος οὐρανὸς ἦνοψ), nor ever did vapor appear, and the sky stretched cloudless" (238.15–16). Here is a truly diaphanous picture of nature.

Later in the poem we hear that "the south wind does not shed so great a pile of leaves, nor the north wind when it comes in the month of falling leaves (φυλλοχόος μείς) as those that the country people then threw around Theseus" (260.11–13). This is a simile which has Homeric echoes but a vocabulary of its own and which may well be taken directly from nature rather than from literature.[4]

In another fragment from the *Hecale* we hear of "ancient cows eating poppy flowers and shining wheat":

βόες ἧχι γέγειαι
ἄνθεα μήκωνός τε καὶ ἥνοπα πυρὸν ἔδουσι.
(277)

This too seems fresh in its observation.

A captivating description of fish comes from the *Galataea*:

ἢ μᾶλλον χρύσειον ἐν ὀφρύσιν ἱερὸν ἰχθύν
ἢ πέρκας ὅσα τ' ἄλλα φέρει βυθὸς ἄσπετος ἅλμης.
(378)

Or rather the holy fish with golden brow or the perch or as many other things that the unquenchable depth of the sea bears.

---

2. K. J. McKay, *Erysichthon: A Callimachean Comedy*, Supp. VII to *Mnemosyne* (Leiden, 1962) 76, sees this passage as derived from Theocritus, *Idyll* VII. Since neither passage can be dated and since the verbal reminiscences are minimal, I do not find his view convincing.

3. Cf. Sappho III.15–19.

4. Cf. Homer *Il.* II.468, 800; VI.146, 147; XXI.464. Φυλλοχόος is not, however, a Homeric word.

16. Wreath of oak leaves and acorns, Archaeological Museum of Thessalonike

There is both epic and lyric feeling here,[5] but the expression appears to be original—and certainly not jejune.

Though the idyllic settings in Theocritus are often described as artificial, resembling presumably those golden wreaths of oak leaves and acorns (fig. 16), olives or myrtle, or the golden spears of wheat from Hellenistic tombs (fig. 17), there is in addition to, or perhaps instead of, such elegant artificiality much of the same feeling for the sweetness of the reality of nature that we saw in Callimachus.

In *Idyll* I the opening lines in their sound match the very sweetness of their sense:

5. Cf. Simonides 567.3–6 and the fragment of the *Titanomachia* cited by Athenaeus vii.277 d:

> ἐν δ᾽ αὐτῇ πλωτοὶ χρυσώπιδες ἰχθύες ἑλλοὶ
> νήχοντες παίζουσι δι᾽ὕδατος ἀμβροσίοιο.

And on it afloat were dumb fish with golden faces swimming and playing through the ambrosial water.

17. Spears of wheat, private collection

Ἁδύ τι τὸ ψιθύρισμα καὶ ἁ πίτυς, αἰπόλε, τήνα,
ἁ ποτὶ ταῖς παγαῖσι, μελίσδεται, ἁδὺ δὲ κὰι τύ
συρίσδες.
                                                      (1–3)

Sweet is the whispering of that pine tree, goatherd, making music beside the
springs, and sweet too is your piping.

The alliteration in π (and ψ), the assonance in α and αι, and the onomatopoeia
in ψιθύρισμα (whispering), μελίσδεται (make music), and συρίσδες (pipe),
particularly with the repetition of ις sounds, reproduce sense in sound.

In *Idyll* XIII Theocritus describes summer as the time when the Pleiades
rise and "the far uplands pasture the young lambs" (25–26, trans. Gow).[6]
Ἐσχατιαί means the "outlying parts of a holding, "[7] and this is a concrete
but, so far as we know, original and picturesque way to describe the beginning
of summer.

Later in the same poem, Theocritus tells us that Hylas, when he went to
fetch water, saw a spring in a low-lying place. "Around it many rushes grew

6. Gow, *Theocritus* I, 97.
7. Ibid. II, 237 on lines 25ff.

and dark celandine and green maidenhair and thriving celery and creeping dog's-tooth":

περὶ δὲ θρύα πολλὰ πεφύκει,
κυάνεόν τε χελιδόνιον χλωρόν τ' ἀδίαντον
καὶ θάλλοντα σέλινα καὶ εἰλιτενὴς ἄγρωστις.
(40–42)

The color terms here—κυάνεον "blue-black" or "dark" and χλωρόν "green" or "quick" [8]—and the words θάλλοντα "thriving" and εἰλιτενής "creeping" give life and so reality to what would otherwise be a merely descriptive passage. They make it not only pretty but sweetly real.

The three nymphs who pull the boy into the fountain are named, and the last of them, Nycheia, has "eyes that look spring" (ἔαρ θ' ὁρόωσα 45). The expression is modelled upon Homer, where warriors "look terror" at one another. As Snell has pointed out, this expression originally meant that they "saw terror" rather than "looked terror," [9] and there are other instances of what either later became or at least now seem to us to be internal accusatives with verbs of seeing.[10] None, however, is so imaginative or so appealing as this.[11] The magic and originality of this expression occur again in the description of Hylas falling "into the dark water as when some fiery red star falls from heaven, headlong into the sea" (50–51).

We do not have in art from this period anything so delicate or so sweet as these pictures of nature, but in the Roman painting of the Three Graces, thought to be copied from a Hellenistic sculptural group of the first century B.C., [12] we have something of the feeling of the Theocritean scene (fig. 18). The Graces dance against a water-green background, actually a grotto with flowers, and have sprigs of flowers in their hands, garlands in their hair. Their flesh blushes on buttocks and breasts delicately but sensuously—like the blush that arose on Pallas' flesh when she anointed herself:

ὦ κῶραι, τὸ δ' ἔρευθος ἀνέδραμε, πρώϊον οἵαν
ἢ ῥόδον ἢ σίβδας κόκκος ἔχει χροῖαν.
Callimachus, *Hymn* V, *The Bath
of Pallas*, 27–28.

O, maidens, the blush arose on her, like the color of the morning rose or seed of pomegranate.

8. See Fowler, "The Archaic Aesthetic," 130–31.
9. B. Snell, *The Discovery of the Mind*, trans. T. Rosenmeyer (Cambridge, Mass., 1953) 4: "The verbs [of seeing] of the early period, it appears, take their cue from the palpable aspects, the external qualifications, of the act of seeing, while later on it is the essential function itself, the operation common to every glance, which determines the content of the verb."
10. See Gow, *Theocritus* II, 240 on line 45.
11. Ibid.: " Ἔαρ is much more imaginative than the nouns elsewhere so used (Ἄρη, ἀστραπάς, πῦρ etc.)."
12. Havelock, *HA*, 268.

18. The Three Graces, Museo Nazionale, Naples

This passage of Callimachus shows the same freshness of observation as do the Theocritean passages, the same sweetness in nature. It also calls to mind the description of Hylas in Book I of the *Argonautica*. A water nymph, rising from the beautifully flowing spring, caught sight of him "blushing with beauty and sweet grace":

κάλλεϊ καὶ γλυκερῇσιν ἐρευθόμενον χαρίτεσσιν.
(1230)

The end of *Idyll* VII seems again to be taken from nature rather than from a literary model, and it surpasses in sensuousness all other Theocritean passages. The narrator and his friends reclined upon deep couches of sweet rush, rejoicing in the fresh-stripped vine leaves. "Many poplars and elms murmured (δονέοντο) above their heads. Nearby the sacred water from the cave of the nymphs fell splashing (κατειβόμενον κελάρυζε)" (135–37). The onomatopoeia of the second word is emphasized by the alliteration in κ of both. "On the shady (σκιαραῖς) branches the swarthy (αἰθαλίωνες) cicadas were busy with their chatter (λαλαγεῦντες). Far off in the thick thorns of the wild raspberry the tree frog kept calling (τρύζεσκεν). Larks and finches sang, the dove moaned, and tawny (ξουθαί) bees flitted about the springs. All was fragrant with summertime, fragrant with harvest. Pears at their feet, apples at their sides were rolling plentifully, and saplings weighted with sloes bent to the ground" (138–46). Words suggestive of color and sound or, in the case of ξουθαί, both,[13] and words meaning "scent" (ὦσδεν . . . ὦσδε 143) enhance the description of this late summer day. Nature here is more than sweet. It is lush. Lehmann has seen these lines as comparable in spirit to the painting of the grape arbor and grotto from the wall of the cubiculum in the house of Publius Fannius Synistor at Boscoreale, and indeed this delicately colored fresco with its glistening grapes, silvery green leaves, splashing fountain, and prettily colored birds, all against a pale blue sky and tawny rocks, does seem, despite its Italian setting, to echo the sweetness of the Theocritean passage (fig. 19).[14]

Apollonius is the most painterly of the major Hellenistic poets, and he in many places comes closest to creating the baroque, even romantic feeling of the landscape painters.[15] There are, however, passages which present the same feeling for the sweetness of nature that we saw in Callimachus and Theocritus. These show too the delicacy of the early lyricists.

When in Book I of the *Argonautica* the Argonauts set sail and the son of Oeagrus touched his lyre and sang of Artemis, "the fishes came leaping (ἀίσσοντες) over the deep sea, mammoth mixed with small, and followed, darting along the watery ways, (ὑγρὰ κέλευθα διασκαίροντες) and as when in the footsteps of the shepherd, their master, countless sheep that have had their fill of grass follow to the fold, and he goes before, playing sweetly (καλά) a shepherd's tune on his shrill (λιγείη) pipe; so these followed, and a speeding (ἐπασσύτερος) breeze bore the ship ever on" (573–79). There is Homeric language here (ὑγρὰ κέλευθα),[16] but reminiscence too of Simonides 567, where "the fish at [Orpheus'] lovely song leapt straight up out of the dark blue sea":

> ἀνὰ δ᾽ ἰχθύες ὀρθοὶ
> κυανέου 'ξ ὕδατος ἄλ-
> λοντο καλᾶι σὺν ἀοιδᾶι.
> (3–5)

What is remarkable in the Apollonius passage, however, is the strong but fresh sense of movement—of the darting fishes, of that chasing breeze.

---

13. W. B. Stanford, *Greek Metaphor* (Oxford, 1936) 54–55.

14. P. W. Lehmann, *Roman Wall Paintings from Boscoreale in the Metropolitan Museum of Art* (Cambridge, Mass., 1953) 114–15.

15. See below, Chapters 3 and 12.

16. E.g., *Il.* I.312; *Od.* XV.474.

19. Grotto and grape arbor from the House of Publius Fannius Synistor at Boscoreale, Metropolitan Museum of Art, New York

Later in Book I, when the Argonauts take their leave of Lemnos, the women come running, "as when bees pouring forth from their hive in the rock hum around the fair lilies, and all around the dewy meadow rejoices, and they flitting from one to another gather the sweet fruit" (879–82). Here again is that distillation of the sweetness of nature peculiar to the Alexandrians. The simile is a painterly miniature, and yet the senses are touched—hearing, sight, feel, and even perhaps smell, for the dewy meadows and the lovely lilies together suggest scent. That the meadow rejoices (γάνυται 881) gives the passage the same sense of starting life that the darting fishes did in the passage above. The lines are not only sweet but vibrant.

In view of the vast amount of ancient literature lost to us, we cannot be certain that any of these passages are unique or modelled upon nature rather than upon some literary forebear. It would, however, be a mistake to suppose that these poets were insensitive to their native or adopted environs—Cos, Sicily, Rhodes, Cyrene, all of which are remarkable for their natural beauty, or even to Alexandria itself, which was built upon one of the most beautiful harbors in the world.[17]

17. For a description of ancient Alexandria see P. M. Fraser, *Ptolemaic Alexandria* I (Oxford, 1972) 3–37; Pollitt, *AHA*, app. III, 275–77.

III

The Baroque

Although the baroque style in Hellenistic art reached its peak in the High Hellenistic period, that is, ca. 250–150 B.C., Pollitt puts its beginnings as early as ca. 380 B.C. [1] He confines the term to sculpture, but the dramatic contrasts, the exaggerated and even distorted forms, and the heightened expressions of emotion that characterize that style can occasionally be seen in the paintings and mosaics of the period as well. Descriptions embracing these concepts occur in Hellenistic poetry as early as the third century B.C. They appear in Theocritus, Callimachus, and Apollonius of Rhodes.

In Theocritus' *Idyll* XXII.8–22, a hymn to Castor and Polydeuces, the account of a storm at sea is quite baroque in its vivid portrayal of opposites. The poet speaks of ships defying constellations that rise and set in the heavens and encountering harsh tempests. The blasts of the storm raise a great wave from stern or prow, and cast it into the hold, and break the bulwarks on either side. All the tackle hangs with the sail, torn and in disarray. There follows a description of the noise of the storm. The wide sea roars, beaten by the blasts and invincible hail. Two lines later the winds abate and a glistening calm lies on the sea. The clouds run this way and that. The constellations of the Bear and dim Manger between the Asses appear again. The conflict of ship with sea, the contrasts of height and depth, storm and calm, light and dark, in this very painterly passage seem to foreshadow the more dramatic of the later Hellenistic wall paintings, particularly the landscape of the Abduction of Hylas from Pompeii, with its stormy dark blue sky, darker blue shadows, and

---

1. Pollitt, *AHA* 111. Havelock, *HA* 113, puts the baroque at 240–150 B.C., while R. Carpenter, *Greek Sculpture* (Chicago, 1960) 208–9, puts it from 160 B.C. on. Bieber puts its height at ca. 250–160 B.C. but, like Havelock, states that it continued into the late Hellenistic period.

20. Detail from the Abduction of Hylas, Pompeii, in situ

its trees and rocks shot through with lurid light (fig. 20). The original probably dated to the second or first century B.C. [2]

Later in *Idyll* XXII.37–50 the description of Amycus is strikingly akin to the baroque in sculpture. He was overwhelming, terrible to see. His ears were crushed by hard fists. His huge chest and his broad back were rounded with iron flesh, as though he were a colossus of beaten metal. "The muscles in his brawny arms stood out beneath his shoulder-points like rounded boulders which a wintry torrent has polished in its mighty eddies":

2. Charbonneaux 391.

21. Seated boxer, Museo Nazionale delle
Terme, Rome

ἐν δὲ μύες στερεοῖσι βραχίοσιν ἄκρον ὑπ' ὦμον
ἕστασαν ἠΰτε πέτροι ὀλοίτροχοι οὕστε κυλίνδων
χειμάρρους ποταμὸς μεγάλαις περιέξεσε δίναις.
(48–50)

This passage certainly owes something to Homer, *Iliad* XIII.137–38, where
Hector is like a rolling stone (ὀλοίτροχος) from a rock face that a wintry
torrent (ποταμὸς χειμάρροος) wrenches from its socket. There the rock is
like the entire man, and the point of the comparison is the speed and force of
both. In the Theocritus passage the simile is more visual, and the comparison,
though it may be less apt, is more particular. The plasticity of the description
of the cauliflower ears and the bulging muscles is again baroque, and of course
we actually have Hellenistic statues of boxers showing these very features.
A striking example is the seated statue of a boxer in the Museo Nazionale
delle Terme at Rome (fig. 21). Theocritus' description of Amycus anticipates

the bulging upper arms, the overdeveloped back, the damaged ears.[3] Other damage to the features of the statue are foreseen in Theocritus' description in the same poem of the boxing match. Polydeuces, stepping into Amycus, now here, now there, gouged him with one hand and then the other. He, drunk with blows, spat crimson blood. All the heroes shouted to see the awful blows around his mouth and jaws. His eyes were narrowed as his face swelled. His opponent confused him with feints on all sides, but when he saw him at a loss, "above the center of the nose, down the brow, he drove with his fist and skinned the whole to the bone" (104–5).

The description of the contest continues in like vein until Polydeuces delivers a blow to Amycus' left temple that splits it open. "From the gaping temple the dark blood poured swiftly. With his left he struck the mouth and his close-set teeth rattled. With ever sharper blows he ravaged his face until he had crushed his cheeks" (125–28). Here is heightened realism to match the most baroque of sculptures.

There is similar exaggerated realism in Heracles' description of his encounter with the lion in *Idyll* XXV. When first he saw him, the lion was going toward evening to his lair, having feasted on flesh and blood. "His rough mane was splattered with blood and his bright-eyed visage and his chest, and he was licking his chin with his tongue" (224–26). When Heracles struck him with an arrow, the beast "raised his gory head from the ground in amazement and looked with his eyes in all directions, searching, and opening his jaws, he showed his ravenous teeth" (232–34). The description of mane, tongue, eyes, and teeth remind one of the vividly expressive and colorful tiger's head in the mosaic from the House of Dionysus at Delos, which dates from the late second century B.C. (fig. 22).[4] Again, Theocritus seems to anticipate the visual arts in his presentation of the baroque. The creature's eyes are wide open, with a large amount of white surrounding the gray-green irises: his visage can indeed be described as "bright-eyed" (225). His teeth and fangs are bared to depict ferocity, though the expression comes close to being a smile—but a very feline smile. The mosaic technique here, which is of closely packed, regularly shaped, many-hued tesserae, alone makes the picture strikingly three-dimensional. The modeling is done by a subtle variation of tints and shades from dark gold to pale pink, from black to gray to white in the tiger's fur, eyelashes, whiskers, and teeth. The insides of the mouth and ears are set off in shades of dark orange and red. We have here the contrasts, the breaking away from a plane, and so the energy of the baroque.

Theocritus' description in *Idyll* XXV of the lion crouched to spring is again vividly three-dimensional, pregnant with energy. "The beast coiled his

---

3. On the date of this statue see Pollitt, *AHA* 146–47, who puts it "somewhere between the beginning of the second century B.C. and the middle of the first."

4. Havelock, *HA* 246.

22. Head of tiger, House of Dionysus, Delos

long tail about his quarters. All his neck was filled with rage. His tawny mane bristled with anger, and his spine was curved like a bow as he coiled all his body to his flanks and his loins":

θὴρ ἄμοτος, μακρὴν δὲ περ' ἰγνύησιν ἕλιξε
κέρκον, ἄφαρ δὲ μάχης ἐμνήσατο· πᾶς δέ οἱ αὐχήν
θυμοῦ ἐνεπλήσθη, πυρσαὶ δ' ἔφριξαν ἔθειραι
σκυζομένῳ, κυρτὴ δὲ ῥαχις γένετ' ἠΰτε τόξον,
πάντοθεν εἰλυθέντος ὑπὸ λαγόνας τε καὶ ἰξύν.

(242–46)

The verb forms ἐνεπλήσθη ("filled"), ἕλιξε ("coiled"), and εἰλυθέντος ("coiled") especially give the picture a third dimension, and the energy of the baroque is in θυμοῦ ("anger"), σκυζομένῳ ("angered"), ἔφριξαν ("bristled"), while the painterly effect is enhanced by the color term πυρσαί ("tawny"). Theocritus next increases the effect of three-dimensionality and energy by a simile that makes the lion virtually spring from the page: "As when some chariot builder, skilled to many tasks, first warms in the fire, then bends, the shoots of the wild fig, which is good to cleave, to form the felloes of a wheeled chariot; and as it bends the smooth-barked fig escapes his hands, and in a single spring leaps far away, so the dread lion launched his whole body at me" (trans. Gow).[5]

Both these passages owe a good deal to their two Homeric models (*Il.* XX.164ff.; IV.485). Theocritus in combining them doubles his effect. In Homer Achilles is compared to a wounded lion that springs and Simoeisios falls like a poplar that a chariot-maker fells and bends to a wheel for a finely wrought chariot. In Theocritus the lion is real, and the point of the simile is the spring of the wood, which Homer does not mention. It is this that gives the Theocritean passage its remarkable energy and a baroque quality that does not appear in the simplicity and speed of the Homeric passages.

Apollonius of Rhodes is generally considered to be the most baroque of the Hellenistic poets,[6] and indeed we can find many passages displaying this quality. In Book I there is, for instance, the slaughter of the giants. "Heracles quickly bent his back-stretched bow and brought them one after another to earth. They lifted jagged rocks and hurled them":

> Ἡρακλέης, ὃς δή σφι παλίντονον αἶψα τανύσσας
> τόξον, ἐπασσυτέρους πέλασε χθονί. τοὶ δὲ καὶ αὐτοί
> πέτρας ἀμφιρρῶγας ἀερτάζοντες ἔβαλλον.
>
> (993–95)

There is movement here—of the back-springing bow, of lifting up and hurling —both vertical and horizontal, and in the jagged (ἀμφιρρῶγας "broken all round") rocks a lifting from and recession into a two-dimensional plane.

The simile that describes the slain giants (I.1003–11) is evocative too of baroque sculpture: "Just as when woodcutters pile long tree trunks just struck with their axes in rows (στοιχηδόν 1004) on the beach, so that, soaked, they may receive the mighty bolts, so they at the entrance of the foaming harbor lay stretched (τέταντο 1006), all in a row, some dipping (δύπτοντες 1008) their heads and chests into the briny waves, their limbs stretched out (τεινάμενοι 1009) above (ὕπερθεν 1008) on the land. Others again were resting (ἔρειδον 1010) their heads on the sands of the shore and their feet in the depths, to

5. Gow, *Theocritus* I, 211.
6. Cf. Körte, *Hellenistic Poetry* 236.

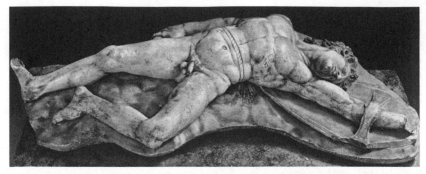

23. Dead Gaul, Museo Archaeologico, Venice

24. Dead Persian, Museo Nazionale, Naples

become prey to both birds and fish." The stretching, bending, and propping of the mighty but dead limbs here are almost sculptured by the language. The picture calls to mind the statue in the Museo Archeologico, Venice, of the dead Gaul (fig. 23) or of the dead Persian (fig. 24), dead Giant (fig. 25), and dead Amazon (fig. 26) in the Museo Nazionale, Naples, in which the prone figures occupy space, exceptionally and horizontally, though they are all too sprawled to suggest tree trunks. Apollonius' giants are clumsier, but that is an aspect of their baroque, even grotesque quality.

The description of Heracles when he has heard of the disappearance of Hylas is equally baroque. He is like a bull, stung by the gadfly, who takes his way, now unceasingly; "now standing still, he raises his broad neck and bellows" (ἱστάμενος καὶ ἀνὰ πλατὺν αὐχέν᾽ ἀείρων / ἵησιν μύκημα I.1268–69). One can imagine the pose in sculpture, and of course the Hellenistic artists did especially anthropomorphize animals. Here the opposite is the case: Heracles is like the bull, but the implication is that the bull suffers like a man. The head of Heracles in the Taranto Museum, which is either a copy or an

25. Dead Giant, Museo Nazionale, Naples

26. Dead Amazon, Museo Nazionale, Naples

imitation of a work by Lysippos and which Bieber and Pollitt date to the third century B.C. (fig. 27), presents a face lifted in suffering as acute as that that the hero suffers in the Apollonius passage.[7]

Apollonius, like Theocritus, tells in Book II of the boxing match between Polydeuces and Amycus, and he is at least as baroque in his account. He accomplishes this baroque effect by a series of striking similes. The Bebrycian king attacked Polydeuces "even as a harsh wave of the sea crests (κορύσσεται) over a swift ship, and she by the wit of a skillful pilot just escapes when the billow strains to rush over the bulwark (ἱεμένου φορέεσθαι ἔσω τοίχοιο κλύδωνος)" (71–73). Polydeuces, for his part, "stood firm and returned blow for blow as when shipwrights with their hammers strike ships' timbers to meet the sharp bolts, fastening layer upon layer, and the blows

7. Bieber 35; Pollitt, *AHA* 51.

27. Head of Heracles, Taranto
Museum

resound, one after another" (79–82). So cheeks and jaws crashed, and there
was a mighty clattering of teeth. Next, they rushed together like bulls fighting
over a heifer. Finally, Amycus rose on tiptoe, like one who slays an ox, and
swung his heavy hand down upon Polydeuces, who swerved, struck Amycus
above the ear, and killed him. The picture of Amycus here is a powerful one
and has the extended pose and diagonal lines of many Hellenistic statues. The
Borghese Warrior is a fine example (fig. 28). Apollonius' passage predates the
statue by about two centuries, but as Havelock says of the composition, "In
the small head and long proportions it is evident that he [Agasias] turned back
to the work of Lysippos. His indecision as to whether to revive the planimetric
composition of classical sculpture or whether to adopt the tridimensional con-
ceptions of Lysippos and his followers reveals a dilemma also faced by many
of his contemporaries." [8]

Callimachus is in general less baroque than Apollonius, but certain passages seem actually to be modelled upon Hellenistic sculpture. This is particularly true of the lines in the *Hymn to Apollo* which describe Niobe, who
ceases to weep at the song of Apollo:

> καὶ μὲν ὁ δακρυόεις ἀναβάλλεται ἄλγεα πέτρος,
> ὅστις ἐνὶ Φρυγίῃ διερὸς λίθος ἐστήρικται,
> μάρμαρον ἀντὶ γυναικὸς ὀϊζυρόν τι χανούσης.
>
> (22–24)

And the weeping rock ieaves off her grief, the wet stone set in Phrygia, marble,
like a woman open-mouthed to shrill some grief.

8. Havelock, *HA* 127 and fig. 98.

28. Borghese Warrior, Louvre, Paris

The words ἐστήρικται "set" and μάρμαρον "marble" in themselves suggest a statue, and the participle χανούσης "open-mouthed" reminds one of the strong expressions of emotion in the faces of Hellenistic statues. Indeed, the Niobe in the Uffizi Gallery, Florence, the original of which dated to the late fourth or early third century B.C., is in her anguish somewhat open-mouthed

29. Niobe, Uffizi Gallery, Florence

(fig. 29). Callimachus may have had some such sculpture in mind, for Niobe appears to have been a popular subject in Hellenistic art.[9]

Even more baroque is the description in the *Hymn to Artemis* of the Cyclopes at their anvils. The nymphs were frightened when they saw them, terrible monsters (αἰνὰ πέλωρα 51) like the crags of Ossa. "All had beneath their brows single eyes equal in size to a four-fold shield, glowering terribly from beneath":

9. See, for instance, Carpenter, *Greek Sculpture*, plate XVIII, "The Stumbling Niobe," from the National Museum, Rome, and the painting on marble from Pompeii of Niobe and her children in the Museo Nazionale, Naples, by the "Boscoreale Master," thought to be after a third-century B.C. original, Charbonneaux 390 and fig. 136.

30. Athene, Alcyoneus, Ge, and Nike, the Great Altar of Zeus at Pergamum, Staatliches Museum, East Berlin

πᾶσι δ' ὑπ' ὀφρύν
φάεα μουνόγληνα σάκει ἴσα τετραβοείῳ
δεινὸν ὑπογλαύσσοντα . . .

(52–54)

Italy, Sicily, and Corsica all cried aloud when the Cyclopes "lifted their hammers above their shoulders and smote with rhythmic swing, snorting greatly, the bronze seething from the furnace or iron":

εὖθ' οἵγε ῥαιστῆρας ἀειράμενοι ὑπὲρ ὤμων
ἢ χαλκὸν ζείοντα καμινόθεν ἠὲ σίδηρον
ἀμβολαδὶς τετύποντες ἐπὶ μέγα μυχθίσσειαν.
(59–61)

These descriptions are exceptionally visual. From both the prefix ὑπό in ὑπογλαύσσοντα "glowering from beneath" and the participle ἀειράμενοι "lifting" we get a sense of vertical and diagonal movement that is reinforced by the adverb ἀμβολαδίς "with rhythmic swing". There is here all the movement, energy, and passionate diagonals of the Pergamene sculptures (fig. 30).[10] It is in a wonderful sense baroque.

10. See below, Chapter 6.

IV

The Burlesque

Burlesque is a mark of Hellenistic poetry and art. The Thorn Remover from Priene, now in the Antikenmuseum, Berlin (fig. 31), which dates to about 100 B.C., is a parody of a late-third-century B.C. statue, probably in bronze, of a handsome, nude youth serenely performing the same task.[1] The terracotta version is of a prematurely aged street boy, perhaps black,[2] somewhat stunted in his growth, with puffed-up cheeks, squinting eyes, puckered lips, and wrinkled nose and brow. He wears a soft beret and a scanty mantle knotted at the left shoulder. There is humor in the parody of the subject matter, but pathos and charm too in treatment. And so it is in the poetry of the period.

Callimachus' *Hymn to Artemis* contains elements of both the burlesque and the grotesque. It is difficult to separate these qualities from others, such as archaizing or the purely playful that is characteristic of Hellenistic poetry and art, but one can perhaps for the sake of analysis make these somewhat artificial distinctions.

In line 2 of the Callimachean hymn Artemis is called the one whose concern is the bow and the shooting of hares (λαγωβολίαι). In the Homeric *Hymn to Artemis* (XXVII.2) the goddess is described in the second line as shooter of stags (ἐλαφηβόλον). In both the *Iliad* (XXI.486) and the *Odyssey* (VI.104) she is also described as a huntress of stags. By making the mighty huntress of stags a shooter of the lowly hare, Callimachus surprises his audience and sets a tone that is not only humorous but also a foretaste of the childhood

---

1. W. Fuchs, *Der Dornauszieher*, Opus nobile 8 (Bremen, 1958); Havelock, *HA* 143.

2. F. Snowden, *Blacks in Antiquity: Ethiopians in the Greco-Roman Experience* (Cambridge, Mass., 1970) 28.

44

31. Thorn Remover from Priene,
Antikenmuseum, West Berlin

scene that is to follow.[3] The playfulness of the whole is enhanced by the very word for play in the following line: καὶ χορὸς ἀμφιλαφὴς καὶ ἐν οὔρεσιν ἐψιάασθαι "the spacious dance and play upon the mountains" (3).

There follows immediately upon this the picture of Artemis sitting, still a little girl (παῖς ἔτι κουρίζουσα 5), on her father's knees and asking him, in her childish imperative, repeated five times, "give me" (δός μοι 6), for her many gifts. These include fifty daughters of Ocean, all of them nine years old, all of them as yet ungirdled girls (13–14). This is in part burlesque. It is a natural part of a hymn to recount a god's childhood—the Homeric *Hymn to Hermes* tells of the baby god's adventures—but it is not a part of the tradition to make a goddess a little girl who sits on her father's knees and calls him "papa" (ἄππα 6) and who stretches forth her hands again and again in an attempt to touch his beard, one whose father in turn laughs and caresses her (26–29). In part this is just the Hellenistic delight in realistic observation and description of everyday life. The lines have the realism and charm of a later

3. H. Herter, "Kallimachos und Homer," in *Kleine Schriften* (Munich, 1975) 378–79, makes a similar point. On the burlesque element in this poem see also H. J. McKay, "Mischief in Kallimachos' *Hymn to Artemis*," *Mnemosyne* 16 (1963) 243–56, and K. J. Gutzwiller, "The Hellenistic Epyllion." A Literary Examination (diss. Univ. of Wisconsin, 1977) 167–92.

passage, which has an element of the burlesque as well. At line 64, we hear
that not even the daughters of Ocean, though no longer little (τυτθαί 64),
could look upon the Cyclopes nor endure their noise. The word τυτθαί is a
part of the theme of childhood and play that runs through this first part of
the poem. The deer at line 100 are, for instance, gamboling (σκαιρούσας).
But, the poet continues, when any little girl (κουράων τις 66) disobeys her
mother, the mother calls one of the Cyclopes to her child; and from within the
house comes Hermes, smeared with ash, to play bogey to the little girl (τὴν
κούρην μορμύσσεται 70), and she puts her hands over her eyes and buries
her face in her mother's lap. All this is from life, more playful than burlesque.
And yet there is an element of the burlesque, especially when the poet says of
the Oceanids' fear of the Cyclopes: οὐ νέμεσις (64). So too begins the famous
line in the *Iliad* (3.156) where the old men on the wall see Helen. It is no cause
for blame, they say, if Trojans and well-greaved Achaeans fight for a long time
and suffer hardship for a woman like this! What follows in Callimachus is not
a picture of the ravishing Helen but of Hermes decked out as a bogeyman.
The playfulness and the burlesque (perhaps in this poem they are one and the
same) continue in the next lines. "But you, little girl, even earlier, when you
were still only three years old (κοῦρα, σὺ δὲ προτέρω περ, ἔτι τριέτηρος
ἐοῦσα), Leto came carrying in her arms. Hephaestus had called that he might
give you birth-gifts, and Brontes set you on his stout knees, and you plucked
the shaggy hair from his mighty chest and pulled it out by force. To this day
the middle of his chest is hairless—as when mange settles on a man's temples
and eats away the hair" (72–79).

If the Cyclopes swinging their hammers in mighty and slanting movements
were a parallel to the baroque in Hellenistic sculpture, particularly perhaps to
the giants on the Pergamene altar, the entire portrait of Artemis in the first
110 lines of this hymn is a parallel to the rococo sculpture which flourished,
especially in Alexandria, in the third century B.C.[4] Children and their pets
were favorite subjects. A particularly winsome little girl is that in the Louvre
seated on the ground and holding a large garland in her hand (fig. 32). One
can easily imagine her charming her papa into giving her all that she asks
for. There is also the now headless statue of a little girl in the Metropolitan
Museum of Art, New York, dressed in clothes too big for her, who holds a
pet in the pouch of her dress (fig. 33). Then too we have terra-cottas, now in
the Louvre, from Myrina of a small boy with a young deer (fig. 7) and a little
girl with a pet hare (fig. 8). All these, but particularly the first, share not just
the subject matter but also the spirit of the Callimachean poem. Artemis, as a
little girl, asks her father for twenty nymphs to tend her hounds, and Pan gives
her two black and white dogs, three red, one spotted, and seven Cynosurian

4. On the definition and dating of the rococo see especially Bieber 136–56 and Pollitt, *AHA*
127–41.

32. Little girl with garland,
Louvre, Paris

bitches. These are, to be sure, hunting dogs, but since Artemis seems still at this point in the poem to be a child, the aura of a child with her pets is in part present.

If Artemis as a child is a burlesque of the usual concept of divinity, the Cyclopes, who are a part of the burlesque in narrative, partake too of the concept of the grotesque, which in Hellenistic art is treated always with sympathy, usually with humor. "They are like the crags of Ossa, and they have single eyes beneath their brows, like a shield of four-fold ox-hide for size, glaring terribly from beneath" (52–54). Hermes, smeared with ash, playing bogeyman, is a more humorous grotesque. More humorous still—and more grotesque—is Heracles, the Anvil of Tiryns, who stands always at the gates waiting to see if Artemis will bring him some fat morsel. All the gods laugh at him, and especially Hera, when he brings from his chariot a huge bull or a wild boar, carrying it, as it struggles, by its hind foot (147–51). This seems almost a parody of Pindar, *Nemean* III.43–49, where Achilles dragged the heaving bodies of lions and wild boars back to the Centaur, for the first time when he was six years old and then ever after. Artemis' being "still three years old" (73) may also be a reminiscence of the same Pindaric passage. The grotesquerie here lies in the contrast between brave little Achilles and enormous, gluttonous Heracles. So greedy is he that he admonishes Artemis with cunning speech, telling her to leave the harmless deer and hare to feed on the hills— they do no harm—and hunt boars and oxen instead (153–57). He wants more

33. Little girl with pet in pouch of dress,
Metropolitan Museum of Art, New York

to eat! Alexandria was, of course, famous for its grotesques in sculpture, but
for anything parallel to this wonderfully funny picture of Heracles we have to
go, not to the realism of those figurines, much less to any of the representations of the drunken Heracles,[5] but to portraits of the sensual satyrs. The head
in the Louvre has something of the spirit of Callimachus' Heracles (fig. 34).
He looks both sensuous and good-tempered—in fact, slightly tipsy.

The first part of Theocritus' *Idyll* XXIV, *Herakliskos*, is, like the opening
of Callimachus' *Hymn to Artemis*, a mixture of the burlesque and archaizing. It
is deliberately reminiscent of Pindar, *Nemean* I and *Paean* 20; Danae's lullaby
in Simonides 543; the Homeric *Hymns*; and many passages of Homer.[6] By

5. For representations of the drunken Heracles see, however, Bieber, figs. 577–80.
6. K. J. Gutzwiller, "Studies in the Hellenistic Epyllion," *Beiträge zur Klassischen Philologie* 114 (1981) 10–18.

34. Head of satyr, Louvre, Paris

using Homeric language especially Theocritus humorously cheats his audience of its expectations. Amphitryon's cry οἴσετε πῦρ (48) is not a demand like Hector's to his warriors to fire the Trojan ships (*Il.* XV.718) but an order to his servants to bring fire from the hearth to light his way to the nursery.[7] The high heroic is transformed to the humorous genre scene. The mighty hero Heracles is shown in his first feat of strength as a delightful infant with a perfectly credible twin brother "who screams and kicks off his woolly blanket when he sees the terrible beasts and their ruthless teeth and struggles to flee" (23–26). There is the usual incongruity of subject matter and treatment.

In the Homeric *Hymn to Heracles the Lion-hearted* (XV) the god is mentioned in the first words of the poem as Ἡρακλέα Διὸς υἱόν "Heracles, son of Zeus." In Theocritus he is in the same position of the line called Ἡρακλέα δεκάμηνον "Heracles, a ten-month-old child." In Pindar (*Nem.* I.35–47) Heracles kills the snakes immediately after his birth. His feat is truly miraculous. Not only can he, a newborn babe, lift up his head (ὀρθὸν . . . ἄντεινεν κάρα 43), but he also has the strength in his (ἑαῖς 45) little hands to strangle the monsters. The deed of Theocritus' Heracles, a ten-month-old infant, is reduced to the amazing.

7. Ibid. 18.

35. Infant Heracles strangling snakes,
Museo Capitolino, Rome

The first day of Hermes' life (Homeric *Hymn* IV) is almost as miraculous as that of Pindar's Heracles, and the account of it is in its simplicity and speed even more humorous. "Born with the dawn, at midday he was playing on the lyre; by evening he stole the cattle of far-shooting Apollo, on the fourth day of the month, the one on which Maia bore him" (17–19). This child could speak, steal, make a lyre out of a tortoise, slay and flay cattle, prepare sacrifice—all in a day's work (17–19). By contrast, Theocritus' Heracles is not such a remarkable baby after all.

In Theocritus' *Idyll* the twins' mother, after bathing them both and giving them their fill of milk, puts them in a brazen shield, of which Amphitryon has. despoiled Pterelaus, sings them a lullaby, and rocks them to sleep (2–5). The shield gives a heroic touch, which is controverted by the tender domesticity of what precedes and follows it.[8]

In the scene that follows, Alcmena orders Amphitryon to get up and not to waste time putting on his sandals. Amphitryon reaches for his sword and calls for light. The passage is full of Homeric language and clearly a burlesque of epic.[9] Theocritus, to make the scene even more domestic, adds the homely detail of the Phoenician woman who sleeps near the mills and who rouses the other servants.

After he has strangled the snakes, Heracles is again presented as a real-life child. He kept showing the snakes to Amphitryon, "he leapt up high in his delight in his boyhood, and he laughed as he laid at his father's feet the terrible monsters asleep in death" (57–59). Alcmena then caught Iphikles, stiff with terror, to her bosom, but Amphitryon laid Heracles beneath his blanket of

8. Ibid. 12.
9. Gutzwiller, "Studies," 16–17.

36. Baby with fox goose
from Ephesus,
Kunsthistorisches Museum,
Vienna

lamb's wool and went back to bed, his mind on sleep. The great adventure ends in a scene of humorous domesticity.

Heracles strangling the snakes had long been a favorite subject of the Greek vase painters,[10] and babies had been important in early Greek literature. Astyanax is portrayed in the *Iliad* very realistically. The babies in the Homeric *Hymns* to Demeter and Hermes are a mixture of the magical and the realistic, and the same can be said of the several babies in Pindar.[11] Babies are seldom portrayed in classical literature, and if they are, they are, like those on the vase paintings, apt to be presented as miniature adults.[12] It is only in Hellenistic times that we have in art babies that look like babies. The statue in the Museo Capitolino, Rome, of Heracles strangling the snakes is a Roman copy of a probably third-century B.C. Greek original. The proportions here are truly childlike, and the rolls of fat around the infant's middle are realistically babyish and perhaps a parody of the muscular adult Heracles (fig. 35). A nicer baby, because it is softer, more fleshlike, is that found in Ephesus and now in the Kunsthistorisches Museum, Vienna (fig. 36). His mouth is slightly open, and he stretches his right hand forth as though he were trying to speak. With his left hand he presses down—and will probably squeeze to death—a fox goose. His proportions, his pose, and the chubbiness of his neck and thighs particularly are all highly realistic, highly appealing. Since this statue corresponds so

10. See, for instance, the stamnos by the Berlin Painter: Paris, Louvre G 192, from Vulci: ARV 208, 160.

11. See B. H. Fowler, "The Centaur's Smile: Pindar and the Archaic Aesthetic," in *Ancient Greek Art and Iconography*, ed. Warren G. Moon (Madison, 1983) 159–70.

12. The children on the miniature jugs made for the Anthesteria are perhaps exceptions. I used to see fat little boys and girls just like these in the Royal Gardens at Athens. See the many illustrations in L. Deubner, *Attische Feste* (Berlin, 1932) pls. 8, 9, 11, 13, 15–17.

closely to one described by Herodas (*Mimiamb.* IV.30–34), it is generally
thought to be a contemporary work and to date to the third century B.C.
The rococo had, as Bieber remarks, already spread from Alexandria to Asia
Minor.[13] The motif of the goose-strangling child, a favorite of the Hellenistic
artists, may in itself be a burlesque of Heracles' labors. Klein saw the statue,
often attributed to Boethus, of the older child strangling a goose as reminiscent
of Heracles' struggling with the snakes, but Herter, more persuasively, sees it
as also patterned after his struggle with the Nemean lion.[14]

The Hellenistic poets treated little girls and baby boys as realistically as
the sculptors of their day burlesqued heroes and gods. By presenting Erysichthon—who in other versions of the story was a giant or a man old enough to
have a grown daughter[15]—as a hot-headed adolescent, Callimachus makes a
burlesque of another hero tale.[16] Erysichthon rushed (σεύατ' 33), for all the
world like a Homeric hero, with twenty giant-men attendants armed with axes
and hatchets against a grove of trees. He smote first not another warrior but a
poplar tree near which the nymphs at noon used to play (ἐψιόωντο 38). This
tree, smitten, called out to the others, and Demeter, noting that her holy tree
was in pain, was angered and said, "Who is chopping down my pretty tree?"
There are Homeric echoes here which set an epic tone.[17] That, however, is
immediately controverted by mention of the playful nymphs and Demeter's
intervention, which is more like that of a fairy godmother than of a goddess of
the *Iliad* coming to the aid of one of her favorites wounded in battle. As she
turns herself into the priestess Nicippe, with fillets, poppies, and a great key
hanging from her shoulder, she reminds one of the Demeter in the Homeric
Hymn (II), but her proper name makes her a figure from real life as well.
Erysichthon, giving the goddess, when she reprimands him, a look more terrible than that which a newly delivered lioness gives a hunter in the hills, is a
blustering burlesque of a Homeric hero. Demeter, for a moment, as she puts
on her goddess form, takes on epic stature, for her steps touch the earth, but
her head reaches Olympus. The giants, half-dead at the sight of her, rush off,
leaving their axes in the trees. This too is a burlesque of epic.[18] Demeter then
becomes more the wicked fairy than Olympic deity. "Yes, yes," she says to
the boy, "build your house, dog, dog, in which you will give your banquets,
for later you will have many a feast" (63–64).

13. Bieber 136–37. On the dating of this statue, see further Pollitt, *AHA* 140–41.
14. W. Klein, *Vom antiken Rokoko* (Vienna, 1921) 30; Herter, "Kallimachos und Homer,"
391. For the statue see Bieber, fig. 285; Pollitt, *AHA*, fig. 132.
15. Hesiod, *Catalogue of Women* fr. 43 a–c; Ovid, *Metamorphoses* VIII.738–878.
16. McKay, *Erysichthon*, and Gutzwiller, "Studies," 39–48, have both analyzed the comic,
especially the mock-epic, elements in this poem.
17. Gutzwiller, "Studies," 40–44.
18. Ibid. 43.

The part of the poem which follows is still more humorous. The exaggerations and the multiplicity of excuses make a mockery of the myth. So hungry is Erysichthon that twenty prepare the banquet for him and twelve pour out wine. His father's folds are empty and so are his byres of four-footed beasts. His cooks have told him "No." Erysichthon has eaten the mules and the heifer that his mother was raising for Hestia. He has eaten the race horse and the war horse. He has even eaten the cat that terrified the vermin. Finally, when he has eaten all the deep store of the house, he sits at the crossroads, begging for crusts and the leftovers from the feast. His parents are so ashamed that when the princes of Thessaly come to invite him to the games of Itonian Athene, his mother says, "He is not at home; yesterday he went to Crannon to demand a debt of a hundred oxen." Polyxo comes to invite him and his father to a wedding. His mother says, "Triopas will come, but a boar wounded Erysichthon on Pindus, and he has been in bed for nine days." Someone is giving a feast. "Erysichthon is out of town." Another, a wedding. "A disc hit Erysichthon" or "He fell from his chariot" or "He's counting the flocks on Othrys" (76–86).

Adolescent boys are for the most part taken seriously in Greek literature and art. The Greeks of the classical period had such respect for the beauty of the youthful form that they seldom made youths figures of sport. Aristophanes' Pheidipiddes in the *Clouds* is a notable exception. We have, however, in the Museo Nazionale delle Terme in Rome, a Roman copy of a Hellenistic statue of a satyr admiring his hind quarters (fig. 37). This may well be a burlesque of a Hellenistic Aphrodite Kallipygos (fig. 38), which we also have only in a Roman copy in the Museo Nazionale, Naples, in itself a satiric statue. The goddess is gazing with fond adoration at her own buttocks.[19] Pollitt sees the many symplegmata—often considered rococo—of satyrs embracing nymphs, Pans pulling thorns from the feet of satyrs, and the like, as parodies of the Pergamene School of sculpture.[20]

There is a delightful burlesque of goddesses at the opening of Apollonius of Rhodes' *Argonautica* III. Athene and Hera take solemn counsel together as to how best to help Jason. Hera first asks Athene to devise some scheme. Athene replies that "she herself has been pondering such thoughts in her heart": καὶ δ' αὐτὴν ἐμὲ τοῖα μετὰ φρεσὶν ὁρμαίνουσαν (18). Not only is the whole scene reminiscent of the councils of the gods in the *Iliad* and the *Odyssey*, but this line echoes a common Homeric formula: ταῦθ' ὥρμαινε κατὰ φρένα καὶ κατὰ θυμόν, "he pondered these things in his heart and his soul." So too, when Athene completed her speech, the goddesses "fixed their eyes upon the ground before their feet": ἐπ' οὔδεος αἴγε ποδῶν πάρος

19. Onians 56.
20. Pollitt, *AHA* 131–34.

37. Satyr admiring his hindquarters, Museo
Nazionale delle Terme, Rome

38. Aphrodite Kallipygos, Museo Nazionale,
Naples

54

ὄμματ' ἔπηξαν (22). Apollonius' audience will surely remember Odysseus in the third book of the *Iliad* who "would stand, fixing his eyes on the ground": ὑπαὶ δὲ ἴδεσκε κατὰ χθονὸς ὄμματα πήξας (217).

The goddesses' plan, once this Homeric tone has been established, is to go to Cypris and urge Aphrodite to order her little son, if only he will obey, to shoot his arrow at Medea and charm her with love for Jason. This is not quite the kind of exploit goddesses in the *Iliad* inspire their heroes to undertake.

The scene that follows has elements of the burlesque and of Alexandrian prettiness too. Athene and Hera come to the great palace of Aphrodite, which her lame husband—himself one of the grotesques—had made for her when first he had brought her as a bride from Zeus. When they come in, they stand beneath the gallery of the chamber where the goddess is accustomed to prepare the bed of Hephaestus. But he has gone out early to his anvils and forge, and she is sitting all alone on a worked (δινωτόν 44) chair facing the door. Her hair falls on either side over her white shoulders, and she is parting it with a golden comb and about to braid the long tresses. When she sees the two goddesses, she rises from her seat, invites them in, and seats them on couches. Then she herself sits down and binds back with her hands her uncombed locks (36–47).

We have a number of Hellenistic statues of women, often Aphrodite, arranging their hair, which does in fact usually fall over either shoulder, and Apollonius may well have had a figure of that sort in mind. A fine third-century example is that of Aphrodite Anadyomene in the Rhodes Museum (fig. 39). The goddess crouches, one knee to the ground, the other raised, her unusually slender body twisted to one side. She is lifting her wavy hair, which here falls behind her shoulders, in either hand, preparing to bind it back. Or Apollonius may, given the detail of his scene, be describing a painting. The description of the "turned" chair and the fact that the goddess is so specifically described as "facing" the door suggest this. The scene, in fact, in its delicacy and sheer femininity, is in spirit much like that on a Centuripe vase of the third century B.C. in Catania University, Institute of Classical Archaeology (fig. 40). Against a rosy background a woman dressed in pale blue with white and yellow swathes of material sits on a stool with a white cushion and turned (δινωτόν) legs. Girls, dressed similarly, stand on either side of her. One, facing, holds a parasol over the seated woman. The other, whose back is partly turned, offers her a fan.

In the Apollonius passage Cypris greets the goddesses: Ἠθεῖαι. This is a Homeric word expressing respect for an elder. So Paris addresses Hector (*Il.* VI.518) and Menelaus, Agamemnon (*Il.* X.37). "Dear ladies," says Cypris, "what brings you here after so long a time? Why have you come? You did not come visiting often before, foremost of goddesses that you are" (52–54). That

39. Aphrodite Anadyomene, Rhodes
Museum

she is sarcastic is confirmed by Hera's reply: Κερτομέεις "You mock" (56).
The rest of Hera's speech and Cypris' reply are quite straightforward. Cypris
is in fact overawed and agrees to do whatever favor Hera asks of her. When,
however, Hera explains what she wants of her and Eros, Cypris says that the
boy will obey them, for he will have some shame before them, but that he has
no respect for her and has in fact threatened her if she dares to take his bow
and arrows to punish him. The two other goddesses "smiled and looked at
one another" (100). One can imagine the quality of those glances and smiles!
Cypris then utters a mother's lament: "To others my troubles are laughable—
nor should I tell them to all. I know them too well myself" (103–4). But she
agrees to coax the child. Homer's goddesses are human; these are feline—a
burlesque of a burlesque.

   The Hellenistic artists were as sensitively attuned as the poets to the ways
of women. A terra-cotta group of the second half of the second century B.C. in
the British Museum, London, shows two elegantly dressed women seated on
a couch and leaning closely together, exchanging confidences of some kind,

40. Centuripe vase, Catania Museum

or perhaps just gossiping (fig. 41). It has again that delightful femininity of
Apollonius' scene of the three goddesses.

Theocritus' *Idylls* VI and XI are the best examples of the Hellenistic
combination of the burlesque and the grotesque. The Cyclops Polyphemus
is himself a grotesque, and his wooing of the nymph a burlesque of a love
affair. The poems have a certain pathos too, for at the heart of the story is the
fairy-tale motif of Beauty and the Beast.

In *Idyll* VI Daphnis sings and tells Polyphemus that the nymph is pelting
his flocks with apples, that she pelts his sheep-dog too, while he has no eye
for her but sits and sweetly pipes. From the sea she flirts (διαθρύπτεται 15)

41. Women gossiping, British Museum, London

with him. "Like the dry thistledown, when fair summer parches it, she flees
the lover and pursues the one who loves her not and moves her counter from
the line"—that is, she leaves no move untried (16–18). The burlesque here is
that the lovely nymph is wooing the ugly Cyclops, and that he pays no heed.
The verb διαθρύπτεται seems to mean to give oneself airs of some kind.[21] It
is not difficult to imagine what sort Galatea assumes. They are in some way
provocative.

In Damoetus' responding song (21–41) we learn that the Cyclops is merely
playing hard to get. He saw, he says, when she pelted his flock, with his one
sweet eye he saw her, his only eye, but he did not look at her. Lately he has
looked in the sea and seen that his beard was fair to see and so was his single
eye, and his teeth shone with beams whiter than those of Parian marble. There
is here the pathos but also the humor of the grotesque in the Cyclops looking
at his reflection in the sea and persuading himself that he is not so bad-looking
after all.

21. Gow, *Theocritus* II, 122 on line 15.

In *Idyll* XI, which is also about the Cyclops in love, we have the same combination of the burlesque and the grotesque. Polyphemus knows, he says in his love song to Galatea, why she shuns him. It is because he is so ugly. A single shaggy eyebrow stretches from ear to ear across his whole forehead. There is just one eye beneath, and the nose is broad above his lip. Still, he tells her, he is in his way rich and talented, and has lovely presents for her. He tends a thousand head of cattle and draws from them the best of milk. His racks are always weighted down with cheese, in summer, in autumn, and in the very worst of winter. No other Cyclops can pipe as he can. For her he raises eleven fawns with collars and four bear cubs. Then the poor creature tells her that she may take logs and burn his soul, his single eye. He wishes that his mother had borne him with gills that he might dive down and kiss her hand if not her lips; he would bring her white lilies or soft poppies with petals of scarlet—one grows in winter, the other in summer, so he could not have brought them both together (30–59). The sentiment here is both awkward and sweet. The invitation to burn out his eye with a log is grisly.[22] The wish that he were a fish and the observation that lilies and poppies do not grow in the same season are childlike. These qualities together contribute to the grotesque.

The so-called Alexandrian grotesques are not really a parallel to the Cyclops, for they are of real people, deformed though they may be. The satyrs that were so popular a subject in Hellenistic art are better parallels to Polyphemus. The probably second-century B.C. group of a satyr with a nymph caught between his knees (fig. 42), the best copy of which is in the Museo Nuovo, Rome, is an example of the same Beauty and the Beast motif. The nymph is clutching the satyr's hair and pushing back his head. His expression is changing from laughter to anguish, not just, as Bieber claims, because she is pulling his hair,[23] but also because of the rejection of his suit. He looks exactly like a child who cannot have what he wants.

A cruder, but perhaps even funnier mixture of the burlesque and the grotesque occurs in Moschus' *Europa*. It is difficult to be sure in this poem how much is deliberately, how much accidentally humorous. It is somewhat like the representation of Europa and the bull on the painted glass goblet from Begram, Afghanistan, originally Alexandrian, now in the Musée Guimet, Paris (fig. 43). A very buxom Europa sits on a very buxom bull. Is it lack of skill on the part of the artist or is he being intentionally funny? I think the latter. This goblet has too the wonderful color—yellow, brown, and blue—and in Europa's "precious gesture and the airy flutter of her scarf"[24] the mannerism of Moschus' poem. The goblet and the poem date from approximately the same period, about the middle of the second century B.C.

22. Cf. ibid. 217–18 on lines 51ff. and 58f.
23. Bieber 147.
24. Charbonneaux 160.

42. Satyr with nymph, Museo Capitolino, Rome

Moschus' poem is a combination of mock-epic and Alexandrian prettiness. It has a unique mixture of Homeric language, [25] lyric feeling, and deliberately awkward syntax. In the midst of the description of Europa's gorgeous basket, for instance, Moschus tells of Io "going the salt waves back and forth with her feet like a swimmer" (φοιταλέη δὲ πόδεσσιν ἐφ' ἁλμυρὰ βαῖνε κέλευθα / νηχομένη ἰκέλη 46–47). Such clumsiness is surely intentional grotesquerie. On the other hand, the picture of the young girls gathering flowers in the meadow by the sea has the lyric magic of the Homeric *Hymn to Demeter*: "One would pluck the fragrant narcissus, another the hyacinth, another the violet, another the creeping thyme. On the ground many a blossom swelled in the meadows fostered by spring. They picked the fragrant down

25. On this aspect of the poem see Gutzwiller, "Studies," 63–73.

43. Europa and the bull, Musée Guimet, Paris

of the crocus cup, and rivalled one another in blooms. The princess in their midst, culling with her hands the glory of the rose with its color of flame, shone as among the Graces, Aphrodite, the daughter of foam" (65–71). This pretty passage is followed by the appearance of Zeus, who "hid the god, changed his form, and became a bull":

κρύψε θεὸν καὶ τρέψε δέμας καὶ γείνετο ταῦρος
(79)

The parataxis, the simplicity of wording, and the very rhythm of the line are, as Gutzwiller has shown, humorous.[26] This certainly is burlesque. "He is not the sort that is fed in the stalls, nor the kind that splits the sod, drawing the well-bent plow, nor the sort that feeds at the head of the flock, nor such that, bound beneath the yoke, draws the well-laden cart. The rest of his hide was all tawny to see except that a circle of silver gleamed in the midst of his noble brow, and his eyes were gray-green beneath and lightninged desire, and equal to one another his horns rose up from his head like crescents of the horned moon where its rim split in two" (80–88). No ordinary bull he!

Not only is the bull handsome, but he smells good. "His ambrosial odor spread afar and surpassed even the meadow's pleasant scent":

τοῦ δ' ἄμβροτος ὀδμή
τηλόθι καὶ λειμῶνος ἐκαίνυτο λαρὸν ἀυτμήν.
(91–92)

One is reminded of Demeter, again in the Homeric Hymn, who put on her own form, thrusting away the nurse's old age; and beauty spread around her, and a lovely fragrance was spread from her sweet-smelling clothes: ὀδμὴ δ' ἱμερόεσσα θυηέντων ἀπὸ πέπλων (277). This heavenly smelling bull then "took his stand before blameless Europa, kept licking her neck, and quite enchanted the young girl. She fell to touching him and wiped the foam from his mouth with her hands and kissed the bull":

στῆ δὲ ποδῶν προπάροιθεν ἀμύμονος Εὐρωπείης
καί οἱ λιχμάζεσκε δέρην, κατέθελγε δὲ κούρην.
ἡ δέ μιν ἀμφαφάασκε καὶ ἠρέμα χείρεσιν ἀφρόν
πολλὸν ἀπὸ στομάτων ἀπομόργνυτο καὶ κύσε ταῦρον.
(93–96)

Again the two sets of tricola, each ending in a culmination of the erotic, are in themselves comical, and the iterative forms λιχμάζεσκε and ἀμφαφάασκε add to the humor. The bull then mooed as softly as a sweet-sounding Mygdonian flute. It is difficult to say whether this is meant to be pretty or funny.[27] What follows is not only comic but, like the lines above, sexually suggestive.

26. Ibid. 70.
27. Gutzwiller, "Studies," 71, sees the comparison as "hilarious."

44. Sow with piglets, Ny Carlsberg Glyptotek, Copenhagen

The bull "knelt at her feet and, turning his neck, gave Europa a look, and showed her his broad back":

ὤκλασε δὲ πρὸ ποδοῖιν ἐδέρκετο δ'Εὐρώπειαν
αὐχέν' ἐπιστρέψας καί οἱ πλατὺ δείκνυε νῶτον.
(99–100)

Here too we have three cola coming to a comical climax. The bull beckoning the virgin to his back with a glance is high burlesque. If it were not so funny, it would be grotesque. The closest in spirit to Moschus' knowing bull is the smug, almost smirking sow with her piglets in a Roman copy at the Glyptotek in Copenhagen (fig. 44). The artist of that piece had a conscious sense of humor.

The humor in the *Europa* gives way for a moment to a scene of true Alexandrian prettiness.[28] The sea grows calm, and the seabeasts frolic at the feet of Zeus. The dolphins tumble joyfully over the surge from the depths, and the Nereids rise up from under the sea, sit on the backs of the beasts, and range themselves in rows. Poseidon himself leads his brother over the briny path, and the Tritons, flautists of the sea, play the marriage song on their long conch shells. Europa sits on the bull's back and with one hand holds on to his horn. With the other she lifts a fold of her crimson dress so that it will not get wet in the foaming sea. Her full robe, billowing at the shoulder like the sail of a ship, makes light work of carrying the girl (115–30). It is the latter part

28. Gutzwiller, ibid. 71, sees this passage as inspired by Homer, *Il*. XIII.27–29.

45. Nereid on sea beast, Taranto Museum

of this scene that the Afghanistan goblet seems to be burlesquing (fig. 43). There the practically nude Europa appears to be using her scarf for a sail. The charm of the passage as a whole, however, is paralleled on a gold and silver lid of the late second century B.C. in the Taranto Museum (fig. 45). There, a slender Nereid rides a fabulous sea-beast. She is nude except for her bracelets and a mantle, which has slipped down to reveal her gracefully curved back and her buttocks. She sits sideways, dangles her delicate feet in highly stylized waves, and grasps the monster about the neck with one arm. In the opposite hand she holds a fan. Her hair is most elegantly done in a "melon" coiffure with a small bun just above the nape of the neck. The sea-monster himself is almost as lovely as she. His doglike head has an open, almost smiling mouth and a glittering red-beaded eye. His spiky mane and erect acanthus tail are matched in imagination by his fantastic, leaflike fins. Soft hairs on his neck turn abruptly to regular scales on a body that ends in an extravagant coil. The scene as a whole is playful, erotic, and simply very pretty.

46. Aphrodite, Eros, and Pan, National Museum, Athens

Moschus' particular combination of the burlesque and the grotesque—a lovely virgin with the mind of a six-year-old child, a sweet-smelling but slobbering bull—is practically unique. The marble group from Delos of Aphrodite, Eros, and Pan, in the National Museum at Athens, which dates to the first century B.C., contains some of the humor of the combination (fig. 46). Aphrodite, voluptuous though she is, seems not to be much aroused, one way or another, by Pan's advance, and Eros himself is merely a pretty child. It is Pan who is most amusing here. He has the face, horns, and hind-quarters of the true grotesque, but he is, as one critic has said, more like an importunate dog than a sexually aroused suitor.[29] The effect, certainly intentional, is amusing. It is, like Moschus' poem, a burlesque of, among other things, Beauty and the Beast.

29. Charbonneaux 316.

V

The Grotesque

Heracles and the Cyclops in Callimachus' *Hymn to Artemis*, the Cyclops in Theocritus' *Idylls* VI and XI, and both Zeus the bull and Io the cow in Moschus' *Europa* commingle the burlesque and the grotesque, but they are all mythological creatures, monsters even, and do not parallel the grotesques of Hellenistic, particularly Alexandrian sculpture. These small figures of bronze, marble, and terra-cotta are of real, usually "low-class," often deformed people, and in their attention to detail of anatomy and expression of face and figure often touching as well as amusing.

Among the subjects of Alexandrian grotesquerie are hunchbacks and dwarfs. Often these are portrayed as dancing, and in fact such deformed people probably did perform in mimes. Since, however, both types are also often represented with exaggerated phalloi, they were probably made as talismans to avert the evil eye. The hunchback is traditionally "lucky," and the phallos was in both Greece and Rome considered apotropaic. The distorted bodies and faces of these figurines may have been thought to divert the evil eye because of their sheer ugliness, or because they provoke laughter, which would in itself dispel the dark powers, or because they somehow anticipated the worst that the eye could do.[1]

1. See D. Levi, "The Evil Eye and the Lucky Hunchback," in *Antioch-on-the-Orontes* 3 (Princeton, 1941) 224–29; H. Herter, *RE*, cols. 1733ff.; W. Binsfield, *Grylloi* (Cologne, 1956) 43–44; W. E. Stevenson III, "The Pathological Grotesque Representation in Greek and Roman Art" (diss. Univ. of Pennsylvania, 1975); H. A. Shapiro, "Notes on Greek Dwarfs," *American Journal of Archaeology* 88 (1984) 391–92. Stevenson holds that many of the so-called grotesques are faithful representations of actual pathological conditions such as Pott's disease and chondro-dystrophic dwarfism. His work is not only valuable in itself but it is also well indexed and provides an excellent bibliography on this fascinating subject.

47. Marble hunchback, Metropolitan
Museum of Art, New York

48. Slave boy with lantern, Metropolitan
Museum of Art, New York

    A hunchback who seems to be dancing appears in a marble figurine in the Metropolitan Museum, New York (fig. 47).[2] His misshapen body is twisted and his overly large head is turned toward one shoulder to suggest this. Here the contrast between the ugly little body and the mature face is touching. The slave boy with a lantern in the same museum may also be a dwarf (fig. 48).[3] The proportions of his body together with the sadness and maturity of his face lead one to think so. A terra-cotta figurine, also in the Metropolitan, is of an ugly little hunchback with bald head, pointed beard, and frowning face squatting on the ground (fig. 49). Again, there is pathos rather than humor in this presentation of the grotesque. Among the most moving and most lovingly made of all the hunchbacks is the exquisite little bronze in the Museum für Kunst und Gewerbe, Hamburg (fig. 50) This African with pigtail, hooked

2. Bieber 96.
3. Ibid. 138.

49. Terra-cotta hunchback, Metropolitan
Museum of Art, New York

50. Bronze hunchback, Museum für
Kunst und Gewerbe, Hamburg

51. Dancing dwarf, Musée Alaoin, Le
Bardo, Tunis

nose, and elongated head seems, in fact, to suffer from spinal tuberculosis, and
the lean and atrophied limbs, the collapsed spine and pigeon chest indicate that
he is near death.[4] He sits cross-legged and holds in his left hand an exaggerated phallos, which suggests that he was a good-luck piece. The expression on
his face is, however, simply heart-rending. The bronze figurine of a dancing
female dwarf in the Musée Alaoin, Le Bardo, Tunis, strikes quite another
note (fig. 51). Her stumpy little body with its large head and buttocks, short,
deformed arms and legs, and little feet and hands thrusts and twists in the
joy of the dance. This is Alexandrian grotesquerie at its best. The delight in
observation supersedes the pathetic.

   We have nothing in the literature of the period that quite parallels these
figures of dwarfs and hunchbacks, but we do have in the *Mimiambi* of Herodas
vivid pictures of bourgeois and "low-class" life. Some of the characters there
do find their reflections in the grotesques and other sculptures of the period.[5]

   In the first Mime, Gyllis, a procuress, visits one Metriche, whose man
Mandris has been in Egypt for nearly a year, and advises her not to waste her
youth waiting for him but rather to accept the favors of a certain Gryllos who
is in love with her. Metriche declares, however, that she will be faithful to
Mandris. Since Gyllis seems to imply that Gryllos will give her money (65),

4. Stevenson, "The Pathological Grotesque," 220–21.
5. Cf. Himmelmann, *Alexandria und der Realismus* 22.

52. Man with Pott's Disease, Fouquet
Collection

it is likely that Metriche is an hetaira. Certainly she is of a higher social status
than Gyllis, for she threatens to beat her. Thrashings and threats of thrashing
seem to be a staple of ancient comedy and should not be taken here as much
more than a comic commonplace, but the threat does say something about the
relative social status of the two women. Metriche tells Gyllis that her white
hairs have blunted her wits, that she would not have listened to such a proposal
from any other woman but would have taught her "to sing her lame song with
a limp" (67–71, trans. Cunningham). Though no one in this poem is literally
lame, it is significant that this is the threat. Lameness was obviously common
in antiquity, and cripples were represented in art as well as in literature. An
extreme example is the terra-cotta figurine from the Fouquet Collection of a
man who suffers from Pott's Disease (fig. 52).

In the end Metriche orders her Thracian servant girl to wipe the black
drinking shell, pour out three measures of unmixed wine, put in a few drops
of water and give it to the old woman to drink. This is a strong potion.
Gyllis at first demurs but is easily persuaded and declares that she has never
drunk sweeter. We know from both Aristophanes and Menander that Greek,
particularly Athenian, women tippled, and we learn here too that women of
Gyllis' class were fond of their drink.

There are in the *Anthology* a number of epitaphs, presumably imaginary, on drunken old women. Antipater of Sidon gives us two which are humorous but not unsympathetic. One (XXVII; *AP* 7.353) is that of gray-haired Maronis, "on whose tomb you see a wine cup carved from stone. She, a lover of unmixed wine and a nonstop talker, does not grieve for her children or their penniless father; she laments even in her grave for this alone: that the wine cup on the tomb is not full of wine." A garrulous, hard-drinking woman, a grotesque perhaps, but the poet views her with humor, not horror. The following (XXVIII; *AP* 7.423) on a Cretan woman tells us rather more about her. "The jug will tell you, stranger, that she was a great talker and the cup that she was a convivial bibber of strong drink. But the bow will show you that she was a Cretan, the wool a hard worker, and her snood gray-haired." Her name was Bittis, and she was someone's wife. A colorful, not unwholesome type—and neither pathetic nor grotesque.

We have in the art of the period two shrewdly observant but at the same time sympathetic portrayals of such drunken old women. Myron's statue in the Glyptothek, Munich, which dates to the second half of the third century B.C., is the more famous of these (fig. 53). The woman sits on the ground, her feet crossed, her knees spread, cradling her wreathed wine jug in her arms. Her head is thrown back to show the sinews of her withered neck. The cheeks are sunken, and the open mouth almost toothless. The expression on her heavily wrinkled face is that of the temporarily benumbed but essentially mirthless drunk. It is clear that the wine jug is the sole consolation of this woman's hideous old age.

Another drinking woman appears on a bronze bottle, now in the Louvre (fig. 54). She squats on the ground, holds an emptied cup in her right hand, and looks stuporous, if not actually nauseated, from drink. Again, the treatment is sympathetic rather than condemnatory.

The head of the Old Nurse, in the Vollmer Collection, New York, is, one might say, tragically treated (fig. 55). Her face is even more harrowed than that of Myron's drunk. Her wrinkles are ridges. She has only one or two stumps of teeth, and her eyes are turned upward in pure anguish. These Hellenistic artists understood and were sympathetic to the horrors of age.

Herodas' Gyllis is not, of course, a tragic figure, but her cunning and her fondness for drink are shrewdly and humorously observed. Herodas, like the sculptors who followed him in the third century B.C., took a sympathetic view of the old woman. A later head, of the first century B.C., also of marble, in the Skulpturensammlung, Dresden, is perhaps more in the spirit of Gyllis (fig. 56). This old woman seems to be laughing, cynically, and her face is not so riddled with anguish and age as that of the Old Nurse. The treatment is, nevertheless, compassionate.

53. Myron's Drunken Old Woman, Staatliche Antikensammlungen
und Glyptothek, Munich

In the third of Herodas' mimes, a woman takes her errant son to a school-
master to be beaten. Thrashings may not accord with our sense of the comic,
but we must accept the fact that the ancients regarded them as humorous. More
amusing to us perhaps are the boy's crimes. He is a gambler: not content with
knucklebones, he plays spin-the-coin. He is too stupid—or lazy—to learn to

54. Drinking-woman bronze
bottle, Louvre

spell or recite. Worst of all, he sits like an ape on the roof, stretches out his
legs and bends over, presumably to see what is going on below. His mother
is not worried about him, but he knocks the roof tiles off, and when it rains,
the whole tenement complains that the leaky roof is the fault of Metrotime's
son, and she has to pay an obol and a half a tile! The woman's husband is,
it seems, feckless—old and deaf and blind. This is a vivid picture of middle-
or lower-class family life, and Metrotime's husband borders on the grotesque.
Again, in sculpture we have frail and bald old men, and we have, too, school
masters and their pupils. A terra-cotta group in the Metropolitan Museum in
New York shows a rather cross old pedagogue with a bald head, a frowning
brow, bulbous nose, hunched shoulders, arms too thin and too short for him,
and a fat belly; he is teaching an undersized little boy to write (fig. 57). There
is also in the Louvre a bald, bearded, stooped old man in terra-cotta, who
is probably a pedagogue: he carries a bag of knucklebones (fig. 58). He has
a deeply wrinkled forehead and a sunken mouth, and his bared chest shows
every rib. His squinting eyes suggest that he—like Metrotime's husband—
neither sees nor hears very well.

In the fifth mime a woman, Bitinna, who has been sleeping with her slave,
Gastron, orders him to be bound and flogged and finally tattooed for his in-
fidelity to her. He at first denies the charge, then begs her to forgive him.
Another female slave Kydilla intervenes on his behalf, and Bitinna relents.

55. Old nurse, Vollmer Collection, New York

56. Old woman, Staatliche
Kunstsammlungen-Skulpturensammlung,
Dresden

This poem gives us an intimate picture of the relations between mistress and slaves and of slaves with one another. The union of free women and slaves in antiquity is well documented,[6] but only here do we have presented the household dynamics of such a situation. Slaves are commonly depicted in the visual arts, and in the Hellenistic period we have more realistic and sympathetic portrayals of them than ever before.

6. See W. Headlam and A. D. Knox, *Herodas* (Cambridge, 1922) xlv–xlvi.

57. Pedagogue and boy, Metropolitan
Museum of Art, New York

Perhaps like the Gastron of Herodas' mime is the terra-cotta from Smyrna,
now in the Louvre, of an old stooped servant (fig. 59). He too looks worn
with toil. His bald, elongated head, large ears, hollow cheeks, and somewhat
deformed spine make him ugly, but the servile, yet intent expression on his
face is haunting. He might be a type too for the shoemaker who appears in
Mimes VI and VII, for shoemakers were apparently considered to be at nearly
the bottom of the social scale.

In VI Metro visits her friend Koritto and asks her where she got her nice
red leather phallos. Metro wants to know where Koritto had seen it. Koritto
explains that Nossis had it. Metro then exclaims in annoyance γυναῖκες—
"Women!" She is annoyed that the friend she had lent it to had lent it out again.
Finally she reveals that she had got it from Kerdon the cobbler, who seems
to be in the business, and she describes him: he is bald and little. Later she
says that she had kissed him and stroked his bald pate, given him a nice drink,
sweet-talked him, offered everything but her body itself to get a second phallos
that he had for sale. In VII Metro takes some friends to Kerdon's shop to buy
shoes. He complains about the high cost of supplies and his large family—he
seems to have thirteen children—but finally gets around to showing his wares.
This is the most fascinating part of the poem, for Herodas, in true Hellenistic

58. Old pedagogue with knucklebones,
Louvre, Paris

fashion, takes delight in detail. Kerdon lists sixteen varieties of shoes. The
care that is lavished here upon the particular is akin to that of the artist who
showed every rib, every vertebra of the small bronze hunchback. Kerdon, the
little bald shoemaker, maker of phalloi, perhaps the lover of Metro (there are
double-entendres that suggest this),[7] is, like the hunchbacks and the dwarfs,
a grotesque. The true grotesques, such as those in the Fouquet Collection,
which seem to be not just realistic portrayals of pathological conditions but
caricatures, perhaps of real persons or at least of recognizable types, catch best

7. See I. C. Cunningham, ed., *Herodas Mimiambi* (Oxford, 1971) 189 on lines 108–12.

59. Stooping servant from Smyrna, Louvre, Paris

of all the spirit of Herodas' mimes. Here in these terra-cottas can be found the like of Gyllis, Kottalos and his father, Bitinna, Kydilla, Gastron, and Kerdon. Their faces are not just physically distorted. They grimace deliberately and are sometimes as wonderfully humorous as their literary counterparts (fig. 60).[8]

The literary and the sculptured grotesques of the Hellenistic period are in general not perfectly parallel. There is nothing in the texts that quite matches the hunchbacks and other cripples of the visual arts. What does perhaps connect them, however, is the phallos. Kerdon, the manufacturer, may, after all,

8. See too P. Perdrizet, *Les terres cuites grecques d'Egypte de la Collection Fouquet* (Paris, 1921), pl. CVII–CXIX.

60. Man with toothache,
Fouquet Collection

have something in common with the apotropaic figurines, for the exaggerated phallos is surely a prime element in the Alexandrian taste for the grotesque. One thinks of the gigantic phallos that was paraded in Ptolemy II Philadelphus' Grand Procession. It was made of gold and measured 180 feet in length. It was painted all over and bound throughout with golden fillets and had at its tip a star of gold with a circumference of 9 feet. This extraordinary artifact was, it is true, a part of the tribute to Dionysus, and its size was undoubtedly a mark of its religious importance, but surely it occasioned laughter, however unseemly, among the spectators.[9]

9. E. E. Rice, *The Grand Procession of Ptolemy Philadelphus* (Oxford, 1983) 20–21.

VI

Passion

Critics tend to think of Hellenistic poetry as artificial and pretty, and while they would perhaps admit to pathos being characteristic of it, few probably would think of it as embodying passion. Yet, Apollonius' *Argonautica* offers subtle but powerful studies of two major passions: that of romantic love and that of remorse. Only Euripides' Phaedra and Medea approach in psychological accuracy Apollonius' portrayal of sexual passion; the presentation in Greek tragedies of remorse may be more profound and more intense than in Apollonius, but it is not more subtle.

Euripides' Phaedra is literally wasting away from love. She is actually delirious. Her symptoms are physical. Indeed her passion is called a νόσος, and medical imagery throughout the play underscores this concept.[1] The physical condition of Phaedra is, however, described only in the second scene of the play—and then briefly. Apollonius, on the other hand, describes Medea's love for Jason in physical and psychological detail.[2]

When Eros had shot the arrow of many sighs at Medea, speechlessness seized her soul. The bolt burned deep within beneath her heart like a flame. She kept casting bright glances (ἀμαρύγματα 3.288) up at Aeson's son, "and

---

1. See B. H. Fowler, "Lyric Structures in Three Euripidean Plays," *Dioniso* 49 (1978) 16–24.

2. E. Phinney, "Narrative Unity in the *Argonautica*: The Medea-Jason Romance," *Transactions of the American Philological Association* 98 (1967) 327–41, shows how Books III and IV are psychologically related; Medea as young-girl-in-love and Medea as witch are really one and the same. J. H. Barkhuizen, "The Psychological Characterization of Medea in Apollonius of Rhodes, *Argonautica* 3, 744–824," *Acta Classica* 22 (1979) 33–48, compares the portrayal here of Medea with those of Pindar, *Pythian* IV, and of Euripides.

her heart within her breast kept panting fast in her anguish; she lost memory of all else, and her soul melted with the sweet pain":

καί οἱ ἄηντο
στηθέων ἐκ πυκιναὶ καμάτῳφρένες, οὐδέ τιν'ἄλλην
μνῆστιν ἔχεν, γλυκερῇ δὲ κατείβετο θυμὸν ἀνίη.

(288–90)

There follows the simile of the poor woman heaping twigs around a blazing brand so that the twigs catch and are consumed altogether. "So did destructive love coiled beneath Medea's heart (ὑπὸ κραδίη εἰλυμένος) burn in secret, and the color of her soft cheeks kept changing, now to pale, now to red, in her mind's distraction" (296–98). Medea has been smitten. She is struck speechless; her heart is pounding; she has no thought for anything else; she blushes and pales. The symptoms are largely physical—and unmistakable.

Later, as Jason left the palace, Medea, "holding aside her shining veil, looked at him with sidelong glances, her heart smoldering with pain (κῆρ ἄχει σμύχουσα). Her mind, creeping like a dream, fluttered (πεπότητο) in his footsteps as he went" (444–47). Again, the images are striking and physical.

When Chalciope asks Medea if she cannot devise some trick to win the contest for the sake of her sons, Medea's joy is again described in very physical terms. "Her spirit fluttered (ἀνέπτατο) for joy within her. At the same time her lovely skin flushed (φοινίχθη) and a mist took her as she melted (μιν ἀχλύς / εἷλεν ἰαινομένην)" (724–26).

That night Medea lay awake, worrying about Jason and the contest to come. For pity a tear flowed from her eye. "And always within pain tortured her, smoldering through the flesh and about her delicate nerves and deep down beneath the nape of the neck where pain penetrates most piercingly when the unwearied loves plant in the heart their torments":

ἔνδοθι δ' αἰεί
τεῖρ'ὀδύνη, σμύχουσα διὰ χροὸς ἀμφί τ' ἀραιάς
ἶνας καὶ κεφαλῆς ὑπὸ νείατον ἰνίον ἄχρις,
ἔνθ'ἀλεγεινότατον δύνει ἄχος, ὁππότ'ἀνίας
ἀκάματοι πραπίδεσσιν ἐνισκίμψωσιν ἔρωτες.

(761–65)

"Her heart throbbed fast within her breast (πυκνὰ δὲ οἱ κραδίη στηθέων ἔντοσθεν ἔθυιεν) just as a sunbeam quivers in a house when it is reflected from water that has just been poured into a cauldron or pail, and now here and now there on the swift eddy it leaps and darts; even so did the girl's heart quiver (ἐλελίζετο 760) in her breast" (755–60). All of this is a realistic and amazingly physical description of the first excitement of falling in love.

When Medea went to the temple to meet Jason, and Mopsus and Argus had prudently withdrawn, "Medea's spirit turned not to other things, singing though she was. But no song that she toyed with (ἀθύροι) pleased her for long in her play (ἐψιάασθαι), but she kept changing it in her distraction, nor could she keep her eyes on her girl attendants but kept peering (παπταίνεσκε) toward the paths at a distance, turning her face (παρειάς literally, "cheeks") aside" (948–53). The iteratives here are especially effective. Other vocabulary (ἀθύροι and ἐψιάασθαι) in this passage emphasizes her delicacy and youth: she is like Artemis and the nymphs. "Cheeks" for "face" suggests her fair and blushing complexion. "Her heart broke within her breast whenever she thought she heard the sound of a footfall or of the wind passing by.[3] When at last Jason did appear before her in her longing, like Sirius from Ocean, beautiful and conspicuous to see but bringing unspeakable suffering to flocks, he aroused in her lovesick suffering. Her heart fell out of her breast, her eyes were misted over, and a hot blush covered her cheeks. She did not have the strength to lift her knees, either forward or backward, but her feet were rooted beneath her" (954–65). These are, of course, commonplaces now, but in extant Greek literature there is no description of romantic love before Apollonius that compares in its physical detail to this.

The simile which follows is, typically of Apollonius, original and charming in its appropriateness. Medea and Jason, when first they meet, stand speechlessly before one another, "like oaks or tall pines which are rooted silently beside one another on the mountains when the wind is still, but later, stirred by a breath of wind, they murmur ceaselessly, so were the two destined to speak in full, moved by the breath of love" (967–72).

After Jason first speaks to her, whether innocently or not, of Ariadne's help to Theseus, Medea is even more enchanted. She casts her eyes downward and smiles with the sweetness of nectar, and her soul, exalted at his praise, melts within her. She takes the charm ungrudgingly from her fragrant girdle and would even have drawn out all her soul from her breast and put it in his hand, rejoicing in his desire. Such a sweet flame does love flash forth from the golden head of Aeson's son. He captures the gleam of her eyes, and her heart warms and melts within her just as the dew melts around roses when warmed by the rays of dawn. Again, the two fix their eyes on the ground, bashfully, then cast glances at one another smiling with desire from beneath their radiant brows (1008–24).

Sappho, it is true, described in vivid detail the physical effects of sexual passion (31), and there are echoes in Apollonius' passages of her language. She, for instance, speaks of the gleam (κἀμάρυχμα 16.18) of Anactoria's countenance; and she speaks of desire fluttering (ἀμφιπόταται 22.12). She also says that a girl's laughter flutters her heart in her breast (καρδίαν ἐν στήθεσιν ἐπτόαισεν 31.6). Sappho's poems are, however, for or about girls, and they are, in the lyric mode, brief in their statements. We have now-

3. Fränkel, however, daggers στηθέων ἐάγη 954, "broke within her breast."

here in ancient literature so sensitive and detailed a treatment of the mutual sexual attraction of a man and a woman as we have here in Apollonius. Whatever Jason's conscious or unconscious motives may be, there can from this passage be no doubt that he is, if not so smitten as Medea, greatly attracted by her—or at least by her passion for him. The closest parallel to this meeting is perhaps that of Nausicaa and Odysseus in the *Odyssey*, but Nausicaa, though obviously attracted, is not, as Medea already is, passionately in love.

The meticulous detailing of the physical effects of Medea's love is matched by the psychological accuracy of Apollonius' account of Medea's dream, which though it may not meet modern psychological standards of probability, is so much more realistic than the obvious riddles and symbols of most dreams in Greek literature that it seems an enormous advance in psychological realism. It really does reflect Medea's wishful thinking and the conflict she feels between loyalty to her parents and her love for Jason. Again, the poet sensitively represents the conflict between Medea's temptation to commit suicide and her natural desire to live when "all around appeared the pleasing cares of life, and she remembered all the joys that the living have, and she thought of her joyful age-mates, as a girl will, and the sun was sweeter than ever before for her to see, since in truth she yearned in her soul after every single thing" (811–16). Apollonius portrays both her youth and her desperation. He is entirely convincing.

The sculptors of the Hellenistic period delighted in figures of adolescent girls dancing or playing ball or knucklebones. A terra-cotta group from Corinth, in the Allard Pierson Museum, Amsterdam, of two young women playing a ball game,[4] is particularly charming, both for the grace of the figures and for the fact that the red coloring of the hair and some of the blue and lavender coloring of the clothing remain (fig. 61). Equally appealing is the terra-cotta from Capua, now in the British Museum, London, which dates to the third century B.C., of two young women playing at knucklebones (fig. 13). The most sensitive portrait of a young girl is perhaps that in the Palazzo dei Conservatori, Rome, from early in the Hellenistic period (fig. 62). She sits with one leg crossed over the other. One arm is braced against her stool. The other she holds in a rather affected attitude across her chest. Her thin, still underdeveloped arm and the dreaming expression on her maturing features tell

---

4. Pollux IX.119 describes this game, called Ephedrismos. Two players took turns throwing a ball or stone at a goal-stone. The one who threw farther was the winner. The loser had to carry the winner on her back to the goal. Often the winner covered the loser's eyes with her hands. In this piece she has just removed them; presumably the two women have arrived at the goal. There are many representations of this game in ancient art. Often the players are young women, sometimes satyrs, and sometimes young women or girls and Eros. See R. Schmidt, *Die Darstellung von Kinderspielzeug und Kinderspiel in der griechischen Kunst* (Vienna, 1977) 129–38.

61. Two young women playing ball, Allard
Pierson Museum, Amsterdam

us that she is, like Apollonius' Medea, at a haunting moment of adolescence. In fact, Apollonius describes Medea, too distraught to listen to Chalciope's questions, as sitting "on a low stool at the foot of her couch, bent over, leaning her cheek on her left hand" (3.1159–60). He may have had a painting or a statue in mind.

In Book IV of the *Argonautica* Apollonius gives us an equally realistic portrayal of the passion of remorse. When Medea and Jason come to Circe's palace, they sit before her like miserable suppliants. "Medea put her face in her hands. Jason fixed the mighty hilted sword with which he had slain Medea's brother Apsyrtus in the ground. Nor did they once raise their eyes to meet her glance. Circe recognized a fugitive's doom and the sin (ἀλιτρο-

62. Young girl, Palazzo dei Conservatori,
Rome

σύνας) of murder" (695–99). Circe knows sin when she confronts it, and we
can assume from the poses of Medea and Jason that they acknowledge guilt as
well as plead for purification.

   After Circe has performed her ritual cleansing, she tells Medea that she
will not long escape the wrath of Aeetes, for he will go even to Hades to
avenge the murder of his son because Medea's deeds are intolerable. In the
end Circe orders Medea from her halls, tells her not to kneel at her hearth,
for she will not approve her counsels or her unseemly flight. At that wretched
pain seizes Medea. She casts her robe over her eyes and moans, until Jason
takes her by the hand and leads her, quivering with fear, outside the palace
(739–52). Medea quails before Circe because she knows she is guilty. In her
shame she covers her face.

   In her speech to Arete, queen of the Phaeacians, Medea openly admits
to having sinned. "Not unwilling," she says, "did I set off from there with
foreign men, but loathsome fear persuaded me to think of flight, when I sinned

63. Bust of Homer, Museum of Fine Arts, Boston

(ἥλιτον)" (1021–23). Later, "night that puts to rest the works of men and lulls all the earth to sleep came on, but sleep gave not the least of rest to Medea, but in her breast her spirit was twisted (εἱλίσσετο) with anguish as when a hard-working spinning woman twists (ἑλίσσει) her spindle through the night and her orphaned children wail around her, widowed of her husband. A tear drops down her cheek as she thinks how dreary a fate has overtaken her. So were Medea's cheeks wet, and her heart was twisted (εἱλεῖτο), pierced (πεπαρμένον) with the sharp pangs" (1059–67).

In Book III, when Medea, in her torment, tries again and again to leave her room to go to her sister and seek her aid, the poet tells us that three times she tries, three times she holds back, and the fourth she falls prone upon her bed, writhing (εἱλιχθεῖσα 653–55). Medea, first in her love, then in remorse, is, literally, "twisted." It is again a very physical description of her anguish. Her passions are contorted.

Passion is a quality that appears in the portrait sculpture that was a triumph of the Hellenistic period. The furrowed face of Homer in the portrait bust in the Museum of Fine Arts, Boston, depicts the passion of the poet (fig. 63). On the silver tetradrachm of 306–281 B.C. the bulging forehead, the full, sensuous lips, and the upturned eyes of Alexander are intended to portray his passionate nature (fig. 64). Sculptured portraits of him preserved these features and added the famous turn of his head to depict his "pothos," the heroic "longing" that antiquity attributed to him. The head from Pergamum,

64. Silver tetradrachm with head of Alexander, British Museum, London

65. Head of Alexander from Pergamum, Archaeological Museum, Istanbul

which dates to about 200 B.C., best shows his heroic passion (fig. 65). Other portraits which emphasize the turn of the neck and the upward gaze are more romantic, even sentimental, in feeling.[5]

Love and remorse are two major passions in Books III and IV of the *Argonautica*, but they are not the only ones. There is also the passion of battle. Jason's contest with the bulls and the earth-born giants at the end of Book III is perhaps even more passionate than Medea's romantic obsession or her sense of sinning. The entire episode is presented in a series of extraordinarily vivid

5. See Pollitt, *AHA*, figs. 16–18.

pictures, which are in their light and shade, relief and recession, baroque in the extreme.

Before the contest even began Idas, in his rage, struck Jason's spear, which he had sprinkled with Medea's charm, with his great sword, but the point of it leapt (ἆλτο 1253) back at the blow (παλιντυπές 1254), like a hammer from the anvil. The picture is vividly three-dimensional and has in miniature the energy of the baroque.

When Jason sprinkled his own body with the same charm, a terrible strength, fearless and unspeakable, entered him, and his hands on either side of him, swelling (σφριγόωσαι 1258) with power, were strengthened. The hands are, as it were, in high relief. Jason then is like a war-horse, eager for battle, "that whinnies and prances and strikes the ground with its foot, and with ears upright lifts its neck high, rejoicing":

> σκαρθμῷ ἐπιχρεμέθων κρούει πέδον, αὐτὰρ ὕπερθε
> κυδιόων ὀρθοῖσιν ἐπ'οὔασιν αὐχέν' ἀείρει.
>
> (1260–61)

"Often, now here, now there, he leapt high in the air (μετάρσιον ἴχνος ἔπαλλεν), brandishing (τινάσσων) his brazen shield and ashwood spear in his hand" (1263–64). Here we have height and depth and auditory as well as visual images. Jason's passion is for battle.

When the bulls come forth to meet Jason in contest, we have not only a sense of height and depth but of great contrasts of light and shade, for they come from out of their unseen lair of earth, wrapped round in murky smoke (λιγνυόεντι πέριξ εἰλυμένα καπνῷ 1291), breathing flame of fire (πυρὸς σέλας ἀμπνείοντες 1292). "You would say that storm lightning flashing from a dark sky blazed frequently from the clouds when they bring their blackest rain":

> φαίης κεν ζοφεροῖο κατ'αἰθέρος ἀίσσουσαν
> χειμερίην στεροπὴν θαμινὸν μεταπαιφάσσεσθαι
> ἐκ νεφέων, †ὅτ'ἔπειτα †μελάντατον ὄμβρον ἄγωνται.
>
> (1265–67)

Jason, "setting wide his feet, withstood their onslaught, as a rocky reef in the sea withstands the waves tossed by countless blasts" (1293–95). Here we have in both the fact and the simile terrific motion and resistance to that motion as well. "Both the bulls, bellowing, struck against (ἐνέπληξαν) him with their mighty horns, nor did they heave him out of the way (ἀνώχλισαν) in their onset (ἀντιόωντες)" (1297–98). Here again are verbs of attack and resistance, of powerful motion.

The simile that follows is again of light and sound. "As when in the pierced melting pot the smiths' bellows of good leather now gleam brightly to kindle the destructive fire, and now again leave off their blowing, and a terrible roar comes from it as it leaps up from below, so did the bulls, blowing swift flame from their mouths, roar, and the consuming heat played about him, striking like lightning" (1299–1305). This is, like most of Apollonius' similes, vivid and appropriate, and as so often, verbs and prepositions give a sense of motion and direction. The bellows and the bulls breathe outward; the fire leaps up; the heat encircles. There is the light of the fire in the furnace and of the flame that the bulls breathe forth, the roar of the bellows and the bellowing of the bulls. There is both the perspective and chiaroscuro of the painters.[6] There is also the recession and relief of the sculptors. The description of sound adds still another dimension to this "painterly" passage.

In Jason's defeat of the bulls we have an even more plastic scene. There are here the exceptionally strong diagonals of baroque sculpture, whether in relief or in the round. "Dragging at the horn of the right-hand bull, he pulled it with all his strength toward the brazen yoke, and threw it to its knees to the ground, striking swiftly with his foot its foot of bronze. So too he threw the other as it rushed him to its knees, smitten with a single blow" (1306–10).

Jason's defeat of the earth-born at the very end of Book III is marked by the same baroque contrasts of light and dark, of verticals, horizontals, and strong diagonals. The giants' first appearance is marked by a simile of light and darkness: "as when after a heavy fall of snow upon the earth blasts of wind scatter the wintry clouds beneath (ὑπό) the gloomy night and all the hosts of stars appear shining through (διά) the dark, so the giants shone, growing up (ὑπέρ) above the earth" (1359–63). After Jason had thrown the quoit, the earth-born "like fleet hounds leaping around (ἀμφιθορόντες) one another began the slaughter, gnashing their teeth. They fell upon (ἐπί) their earth mother beneath (ὑπό) their own spears, like pines or oaks, which gusts of wind shake" (1373–76). Here in the picture of the falling giants we have, reinforced by the prepositions, a strong sense of verticals, horizontals, and diagonals. This scene is followed immediately by another simile which gives again a picture of light and darkness. Jason "like a fiery star that leaps from heaven blazing a furrow of light, a portent to men who see it shooting with a gleam through the dusky sky" (1377–79), rushed upon the earth-born men. He drew his sword and smote, "mowing them down on all sides, many in the belly or in their sides that were half risen to the air, some that had risen as high as the shoulders, and some that had just stood upright" (1381–84). Jason pressed on with his slaughter, and the giants "fell, some on their faces, biting the rough clod of earth with their teeth, some on their backs, others on the flats of their hands and their sides, like sea-monsters to see" (1393–95). We have gone, once more, from a scene of light and dark to one of verticals and horizontals, from a painterly to a sculptural presentation.

In these last passages the passion of battle is marked by contrasts of light and shade, of vertical and horizontal positions. In Roman wall paintings

6. See Chapter 12, below.

assumed to be copies of Hellenistic originals we have too a baroque chiaroscuro which suggests an interest in what is viewed as passionate nature. The
Pompeian wall painting, the Abduction of Hylas, is an example (fig. 20).
Another is the rocky landscape with the pastoral scene of a man leading a
ram, also from Pompeii and now in the Museo Nazionale, Naples, where
gray and rose-colored rocks are piled, artificially, into a mountainous background (fig. 76). In the foreground are some architectural elements and behind
these a distorted tree growing at an unlikely angle. The sky, of blues, greens,
and grays, the mountain, and the foreground are all highlighted by a fantastic, distorting light. One might well be in the midst of a thunderstorm. The
effect is eerie, more than realistic; it is suprareal, a really romantic landscape
which quite parallels the magic of Apollonius' similes. The original painting
is thought to date to the second century B.C., approximately a hundred years
after the publication of the *Argonautica*.

Apollonius seems also to have preceded in his baroque rendering of passion the sculptors of the Hellenistic period, for more than anything else the
large frieze on the Great Altar of Zeus from Pergamum, now in the Staatliches
Museum, East Berlin (fig. 30), pulses with the passion of Jason's battle with
the bulls and the earth-born giants. Here in a frieze more than two meters
high, striding Olympians, often marked with bestial attributes—lions, horses,
dogs, snakes—attack giants who are in themselves part bestial (figs. 66, 67).
Some of them have legs that end in monstrous scaly snakes with open mouths,
pointed teeth, and evilly expressionless eyes. One giant has above a thickening
neck and shoulders the horns of a bull; another, the head and paws of a lion.
Certain giants, gods, and goddesses wear magnificent wings which help to fill
the already crowded surface of the frieze and contribute to the terrific sense of
motion and power that we get from the attacking and battling figures.

The gods and goddesses and particularly the giants on this great frieze
are presented to us largely as a series of torsoes in back or frontal view. Their
musculature is greatly exaggerated, and they are carved in such high relief
that they appear almost to be in the round. Almost all motion is toward the
left or the right so that the figures form diagonals which alternately diverge
and collide. This pattern of action is reminiscent of Jason's wrestling with the
bulls, where his forcing of them to the ground presented strong diagonals, and
of his slaying of the giants who fell like oaks and pines, prone, on the flats
of their hands, and on their sides. The falling in itself must have constituted
diagonals, and the simplicity of the positions in which they fell is not unlike
the full front or full rear views we have in the Pergamene frieze. We have there
too the figure of Ge, risen from the earth like some of the giants, only to just
below her breasts (fig. 30).

The passion of the battle is expressed in the Great Altar of Zeus not only
in the contorted poses, fantastic wings, and swirling draperies of the striding
and wrestling figures of gods and giants but in the anguished expressions of

66. Aether battling lion-headed giant, from the Great Altar of Zeus at
Pergamum, Staatliches Museum, East Berlin

the faces. The giant Alcyoneus, whom Athene is lifting by the hair while her
snake, coiled around her left arm and behind his torso, bites his right breast,
is an especially good example. Even his writhing locks suggest his torment,
which is reflected in the face and hair of his mother Ge, who lifts her hands in
horror at the deed. One can imagine in these anguished but beautiful faces the
torment not only of Jason and the earth-born giants but of Medea in her love
and remorse.

The serpents of the great Pergamum frieze have their parallel too in
Book IV of the *Argonautica*. Apollonius, like the sculptors, seems to have
been attracted by the creatures. He first mentions Ladon, the serpent that had
kept watch over the golden apples in the garden of Atlas. When the Argonauts
arrived, he lay, smitten by Heracles, at the trunk of the apple tree, and only
the tip of his tail writhed (σκαίρεσκεν, literally "skipped," 1402). From his
head down his dark spine he lay lifeless. Later Mopsus stepped upon a dread
serpent which lay in the sand to escape the noonday heat, too sluggish to

67. Snake-legged giant, from frieze of the Great Altar of Zeus at
Pergamum, Staatliches Museum, East Berlin

attack of its own will an unwilling foe, nor would it dart full face at one who
gave ground. But when Mopsus trod upon the end of its spine, writhing round
in its pain (πέριξ ὀδύνῃσιν ἑλιχθείς 1520), it bit and tore the flesh between
the shin bone and the muscle. The word for writhing is the same as that that
was used of Medea in her agony. It also describes very well the serpents of the
great Pergamum frieze.

In the simile describing how the Argo sought an outlet from the Tritonian
Lake, Apollonius gives us another picture of a snake. "As a serpent goes
writhing (εἱλιγμένος) along his crooked (σκολιήν) path (1541) when the
fiercest blaze of the sun warms him, and with a hiss turns his head, now this
way, now that, and in his fury his eyes gleam like sparks of fire until he slithers
into his lair through a cleft in the rock," so did Argo wander for a long while.

On the Pergamum frieze Poseidon's chariot is drawn by sea horses; their
forequarters are fins. In the *Argonautica* Triton, when he appears in his true
form, is from the top of his head, around his back and waist as far as the
belly, wonderfully like the blessed ones in form, but below his flanks a forked
tail of a sea-monster—as such were the fallen giants in Book III described—
lengthened out on this side and on that. He strikes the surface of the sea with
spines, which are divided below into curving fins like the horns of the moon
(1610–16). Again, Apollonius seems to have anticipated in imagination the
Pergamene sculptors.

VII

Pathos

Many of the epitaphs of Book VII of the *Anthology* are humorous, but many others by their very function are pathetic. The deaths of babies, children, and young women are especially common themes. Antipater of Sidon XXI (*AP* 7.164) tells of Prexo of Samos, whose husband Theocritus erected her tomb. She died in the pains of labor at twice eleven years and left behind her a little boy Calliteles, three years old, still an infant. The same author (LIII; *AP* 7.464) tells of Aretemias, who set foot on the strand of Cocytus carrying one of the twins she bore; the other she left with her husband Euphron. Dioscorides (XXXIX; *AP* 7.166) gives an epitaph for Lamisca of Samos, who breathed her last in the grievous pains of labor and whom now the shores of Libya beside the Nile bury with her twin babies. She was twenty years old. In Dioscorides XL (*AP* 7.167) Polyxena tells us that she was the wife of Archelaus, daughter of Theodectes and Demarete, a mother too insofar as her labor went, for fate overtook her child before it was twenty days old, and she herself died at eighteen—for a short time a mother, for a short time a bride, in all short-lived.

Both the theme of death in childbirth and the pathos of it is portrayed in the painted marble Hediste stele from Demetrias, Thessaly, now in the Volos Museum (fig. 68). This, since it is one of the few original Greek Hellenistic paintings, is particularly valuable for our study. Hediste herself, who has apparently just died, lies slightly turned toward us so that we have almost a full view of her face, which reveals even in death her recent suffering, and a view too of her only slightly covered, full breasts, which suggest to us her youth, her wasted sexuality, and her frustrated motherhood. This three-quarter view of Hediste, which differs in its perspective from that of the other figures in the scene, in itself creates pathos. Parts of her pillow, her face, and her breasts

68. Hediste stele, Volos Museum

are accentuated by a play of light that contrasts significantly with the shadows, which create not only perspective but a sense of the sorrow of death.

A stele-shaped loculus slab from the Soldier's Tomb from the Ibrahimiya Cemetery at Alexandria, now in the Metropolitan Museum, New York, shows a woman dying in childbirth (fig. 69). Supported on the right by a small girl holding her under the left arm, she falls backward onto a couch. The dying woman is naked except for her bright yellow shoes and a garment, draped across her knees, of deep red bordered with lavender. The couch is covered

69. Woman dying in childbirth, Metropolitan Museum of Art, New York

with a white cloth. The flesh of the women is tan, their hair dark brown, and
both the attending women seem to be dressed in brown. The style is that of
the First Period of Ptolemaic painting and closely resembles its fourth-century
Attic prototypes.[1] Even in its abraded condition one senses in the slant of the

1. B. R. Brown, *Ptolemaic Paintings and Mosaics and the Alexandrian Style* (Cambridge,
Mass., 1957) 20.

70. Young woman and naked baby, Graeco-Roman Museum, Alexandria

dying woman's body, the curving lines of her arms, repeated in the curves of
her breasts, of the draped garment, and of the top of her head the pathos of
this death in childbirth.

Other Alexandrian tomb paintings show both men and women saying
farewell to children, but a funerary slab from an unknown region, now in
the Graeco-Roman Museum at Alexandria, which is in better condition than
some, shows a young woman seated on a stool; she leans slightly forward and
stretches out a hand to a naked baby which kneels on the floor before her
(fig. 70). This is later than the painting of the woman dying in childbirth and

71. Bearded man and two children, Graeco-Roman Museum, Alexandria

falls in Style III of Ptolemaic painting. Presumably this woman has died and
left an infant behind her. The painting does not have the grace of the Style I
stele from the Shatbi Cemetery on which a bearded man, seated on a rock,
strokes the head of a small child who stands at his knee, while a second, naked
child crawls toward him holding out its right arm (fig. 71). It is the father here,

one assumes, who has died. The curvilinear conception of his entire body matches the pathos of the epigrams from the *Anthology*. The woman of the Style III painting is comparatively rigid and quite separated in the composition from her child.

Another theme in the epitaphs of the *Anthology* that particularly arouses pity is the death of infants and youths. Antipater of Sidon (XXVI; *AP* 7.303) gives us one on little Cleodemus, still living on milk, who put his foot outside the edge of the ship; the truly Thracian Boreas cast him into the sea, and the wave quenched his baby's soul. Again, Diotimus (IV; *AP* 7.261) asks, What use is it to labor in childbirth, what use to bear children, if she who bears them is to see them dead? For his mother built a tomb for her young (ἠιθέῳ) Bianor, but it was fitting for him to build it for her. Bianor had, it seems just reached manhood. In these epitaphs, as in the art of the period, we have combined a compassion for mothers in childbirth and a sense of the waste of death in the early years.

Common too in the *Anthology* are epitaphs on young girls who have died before their time. Diotimus (V; *AP* 7.475) gives us an especially pitiable tale. Scyllis went to the house of her father-in-law, lamenting the death of her bridegroom Evagoras. Nor did that poor widowed girl return to her father's house, for she died three months later in a deadly wasting away of her soul. Sadder still, to the ancients at least, was the death of a girl before her marriage. Antipater of Sidon (LVI; *AP* 7.711) tells of Clinareta, whose saffron couch had already been spread within the golden wedding chamber. Her parents were hoping to kindle the pine torch, holding it on high with both hands. But sickness snatched the girl and led her away to the sea of Lethe. Now her girl companions beat not at her door but their breasts in the sounding ritual of death. Anyte, a woman herself, expresses the same sentiment. In V (*AP* 7.486) she says that often on this tomb of her daughter did the mother Cleina call on her short-lived child, summoning back the soul of Philainis, who before her wedding crossed the pallid river of Acheron.

A funerary slab from the Hadra cemetery in the Graeco-Roman Museum, Alexandria—inscribed "Asia, an Istrian"—shows a preliminary drawing of a woman, surely the departed, seated on a stool (fig. 72). The slender grace of the figure tells us that she is young, and the curved body, her drooping head, and the sad expression of her face, that she is dead. She belongs to the Ptolemaic Style II and reflects the pathos of the epitaphs on young women which belong to approximately the same period, the third century B.C.

Children are, like young women and infants, an obvious subject for pathos, and Theocritus and Callimachus both exploit the theme in their epigrams. In XVI Theocritus tells of a child who went to her death in her seventh year, for she grieved for her brother, an infant of twenty months. In XX he tells of little Medeius, who built a tomb for his Thracian nurse and inscribed upon it "Cleita's." So will she be thanked for her rearing of him, for she will

72. "Istria, an Asian," Graeco-Roman Museum, Alexandria

be called "good." Callimachus' brief elegy (XIX) is perhaps his most moving: "Here the father Philippus laid his twelve-year-old son, his great hope, Nicoteles." [2] The next (XX) lacks the simplicity of XIX and is more obvious though successful in its attempt to arouse pathos: "In the morning we buried Melanippus. As the sun set, the maiden Basilo died by her own hand, for she could not bear to place her brother on the pyre and live. The house of her father Aristippus saw a twofold sorrow, and all Cyrene bowed her head as she saw the house fortunate in its children left desolate." Callimachus uses too the theme of the old nurse. In another epigram (L) Miccus cared for "Phrygian Aeschre, his good nurse, in her old age, with all good things, for as long as

2. See Ferguson, "The Epigrams of Callimachus," 64–80, on the pathetic effects of this poem.

73. Nurse and child, Metropolitan Museum of
Art, New York

she lived, and when she died, he set up this tomb for all who come after to see,
so that the old woman has his thanks for her breasts." Children and old women
were a triumph of Hellenistic art. We have in the Metropolitan Museum, New
York, a "grotesque" terra-cotta of a short, ape-faced old nurse carrying an
oversized little girl (fig. 73). The woman's very ugliness is pathetic.

Old men and old women are in other contexts also a subject for pathos
in the *Anthology*. Asclepiades XXXIII (*AP* 13.23) gives us an epigram on
Botrys: "Passerby, even if you are in a hurry, listen to the exceeding grief
of Botrys. An old man of eighty years, he buried his son of nine, already
speaking with some skill and wisdom." The theme of the inappropriateness
of the old burying the young is common in antiquity, but here the extremes of
age in father and son increase the pathos of the topos. More fortunate were

the eighty-year-old twin women, priestesses in their time, in Diotimus VI (*AP* 7.733); they wanted but nine days to complete their eightieth year. They loved their husbands and children, and they, old women, went to Hades before them. Leonidas of Tarentum LXXII (*AP* 7.726) writes of the death of an eighty-year-old spinning woman. "Often had she thrust sleep away from her, morning and evening, to ward off poverty. She used to sing to her spindle and help-mate distaff, and by the loom until the dawn she spun with the Graces that long task of Athene, or with wrinkled hand on wrinkled knee smoothed thread sufficient for the loom, a lovely (ἱμερόεσσα) woman. At eighty years, beautiful Platthis, who wove so beautifully, beheld the waters of Acheron." It is comforting to know that not all old women, not even those who had to work for their living, were considered grotesques. Asclepiades XLI (*AP* 7.217), in fact, tells us of a courtesan who was desirable even in her old age. He speaks in the person of her tomb. "I hold Archeanassa, the hetaira from Colophon, even on whose wrinkles sweet love sat. O Lovers who plucked the fresh flower of her first youth, through what a furnace you passed!" These old women are pitiable only in their old age and in their deaths; their lives seem not to have been so bad.

Another subject for pathos is that of the unknown dead. Leonidas of Tarentum LXIII (*AP* 7.478) asks: "Who ever are you? Whose poor bones are these that remain beside the road, bare, in a coffin half-open to the light? The monument and the tomb are ever grazed by the axle and the wheel of the way-farer's coach. Soon the wagons will crush your ribs, poor wretch, and no one will shed a tear for you." Callimachus LVIII writes on a shipwrecked stranger: "Who are you, O shipwrecked stranger? Leontichus found you here, a corpse upon the beach. He covered you in this tomb, weeping for his own doomed life, for he has no rest either, but like a gull roams the sea." This is doubly pathetic, for Leontichus sees his own life in the death of the shipwrecked sailor.

There are in the *Argonautica* of Apollonius of Rhodes flashes of pathos. In Book I Jason's mother, saying goodbye to him, "cries as a girl all alone cries, fondly embracing her white-haired nurse, for she has no others to care for her but leads a toilsome life beneath a stepmother who insults her with ever fresh reproaches, and her heart within as she weeps is bound with woe, nor can she sob forth all the sorrow that struggles to break forth" (269–75). Later in the same book Apollonius describes Hypsipyle's nurse as rising, "limping for very age upon her shrivelled feet, leaning on a staff, and eager to speak":

> γήραϊ δὴ ῥικνοῖσιν ἐπισκάζουσα πόδεσσιν,
> βάκτρῳ ἐρειδομένη, πέρι δὲ μενέαιν' ἀγορεῦσαι
>   (669–70)

This is an exceptionally vivid picture of an old woman. In Book III Medea's heart melting in love for Jason is like "a woman that spins for daily hire (χερνῆτις) who heaps up dry twigs around a blazing brand, whose task is the spinning of wool, so that she may kindle a light beneath the roof at night, when she wakes very early, and a wondrous [flame] from a little brand consumes all the twigs" (291–95). This is an Alexandrian "genre scene," but the picture of the poor working woman who must rise before dawn to spin her wool is one of pathos. More piteous still is the brief mention, in a description of night, of deep sleep wrapping round a mother whose children are dead (καί τινα παίδων / μητέρα τεθνεώτων ἀδινὸν περὶ κῶμ᾽ ἐκάλυπτεν III.747–48).

In Book IV Medea, weeping as she leaves home, is like "a handmaid stealing away from a rich house, whom fate has recently separated from her native land, nor has she yet made trial of wretched toil but unaccustomed to misery and distraught with fear at slavish tasks goes about beneath the harsh hands of her mistress" (35–39). Apollonius shows the same pity for slaves as do the sculptors of the period. Later in Book IV, Medea at the court of Arete and Alcinous, in danger of being surrendered to the Colchians, is in her anxiety "like a toiling woman who turns her spindle all night long, and around her, widowed of her husband, her orphaned children wail. Tears drop down her cheeks as she thinks of how painful a fate has taken her" (1062–65). Widows and orphans arouse the poet's pity, and nowhere do we see this mood more clearly than in the curious simile that describes Medea's anguish in Book III. As she tries to make up her mind to leave her bedroom to go to her sister, she is, says the poet, "like a bride who in her chamber weeps for her young husband, to whom her brothers and parents have given her, nor does she yet mingle at all with all her maidservants, for shame and for thinking of him, but grieving she sits apart. Some doom destroyed him before they enjoyed one another's charms. She, kindled within, weeps in silence as she looks upon her widowed bed, in fear that the women will mock and scoff at her" (656–63). The reason for the women's almost incomprehensible mockery is presumably the fact that the marriage had not been consummated before the bridegroom's death. Although this seems cruel to us, there is no question of the general tone of pathos that Apollonius intends to create.

The sculptors and the painters of the Hellenistic age treated the same subjects as the poets: the death of babies, children, young women; slaves, working women, old women, widows, and orphans. The old market woman in the Metropolitan Museum, New York, and the old shepherdess in the Palazzo dei Conservatori, Rome, are good examples of poor, toiling women, and they are both treated with compassion—and realism.[3] They do not, however, evoke the same sense of pathos that the epigrammatists and especially Apollonius do in their verse. For that we must turn to the limestone statue of a young boy, found in the ancient necropolis of Tarentum and now in the Staatliches Museum, Berlin, which dates to about 300 B.C. (fig. 74). His cropped hair and

3. Bieber, 141 and figs. 590–91.

74. Slave boy from Tarentum, Staatliches Museum, East Berlin

short, belted exomis make his slave status clear, and his features—a wide, flat head, flat nose, and full, protruding lower lip—suggest that he is a foreigner. His stooping posture reveals that he has had a laborious life. He stands gazing with sadness and devotion, presumably at his dead master, a touching figure indeed. We must look, too, to the bronze torso of Demeter in the Archaeological Museum, Izmir, Turkey, which dates to the third century B.C. (fig. 75).

75. Demeter, Archaeological Museum, Izmir

The latter expresses surely the goddess's grief at the loss of her daughter Perse-phone. The slightly inclined head, the deep-set eyes, pulled slightly upward at the inner corners by the anxious brow, express the anguish of loss. This goddess suffers no more and no less than the bereaved women of Apollonius' similes—the widows and mothers whose children are dead.

VIII

The Pathetic Fallacy

Akin to the mood of pathos in Hellenistic poetry and art is the pathetic fallacy, which, as far as we know, makes its first real appearance in Theocritus' *Idyll* I. Where were you, Thyrsis, ask the nymphs, when Daphnis was dying? "For him the jackals howled; for him, the wolves. For him when he died even the lion of the forest wept. Many cows about his feet, and many bulls, many heifers and calves, made lament" (71–75). The wild animals as well as the kine that Daphnis tended mourn at his death. The poet here openly attributes to the animal kingdom human sentiment. Daphnis himself in his farewell to the wolves, the jackals, and the bears in their mountain caves implies, though he does not state, a similar identification of man and beast. Thyrsis at the end of his song proposes an *adynaton* that has its precedent in Archilochus (Diehl 74) but which differs from it considerably in tone and circumstance. Archilochus is referring to an actual eclipse of the sun. If that can happen, he says, if Zeus can hide the sun and make night from noon, let no one be surprised if wild beasts change places with dolphins; if the echoing waves of the sea become dearer to beasts than the dry land, and the wooded mountains to dolphins. This is a literary conceit, charming but devoid of any sentiment but that of surprise. When Thyrsis invites nature to mourn at the death of Daphnis, there is, however, both sweetness and sorrow: "Bear violets now, O brambles, bear violets, thorns, and let the lovely narcissus bloom on juniper trees .˙. . let the pine bear pears since Daphnis is dying. Let the stag drag the hounds, and from the mountains let the owls sing to nightingales" (132–36). This *adynaton* has become the pathetic fallacy. There is an echo of the same story and another instance of the pathetic fallacy in *Idyll* VII. Tityrus will sing of "how once

Daphnis the cowherd loved Xenea, and how the mountain sorrowed for him and how the oaks that grow on the river Himera's banks lamented him, when he was wasting like any snow beneath high Haemus or Athos or Rhodope or the farthest Caucasus" (73–77). The mention of real mountains enhances the pathos of the fiction.

The pathetic fallacy next appears in texts left to us from about a century later. It occurs there in laments for both imaginary, that is, mythological, and historical persons. Theocritus' literary conceits have been adapted to both. A surprising and moving example occurs in Antipater of Sidon's epitaph (XXV; *AP* 7.241) for a dead prince, one of the Ptolemies, possibly Philometor's son Eupater, who died about 150 B.C.[1] We know from the epigram itself that he died in an epidemic and that his death was followed by an eclipse of the moon. It is not surprising, then, that the pathetic fallacy appears here. His father and his mother, the poet tells us, again and again defiled their hair, and afterwards his tutor bewailed him, gathering in his soldier's hands the dark dust to pour over his head. "Mighty Egypt plucked out her hair, and the broad home of Europa groaned, and the Moon herself, darkened by grief, abandoned the heavenly paths and the stars." That this brief twelve-line poem refers to a real prince and a real eclipse of the moon increases the effectiveness of the pathetic fallacy.

Bion's *Lament for Adonis* is for a mythological figure, and its tone is more sensual than sad. It breathes sweet decay and is indeed more akin to Rimbaud and Baudelaire than it is to Theocritus or to the pastoral tradition that follows him. The red blood that drips down to Adonis' white flesh, the rose that flees from his lips, the kiss itself that dies, that Cypris will never have—the kiss of the dead would suffice, but, he does not know that she has kissed him, dead (9–14)—all this sounds more like *Fleurs du mal* than it does like Theocritus. The refrain, repeated from line 6 above, reflects in its sound the shrill wailing of grief (αἰάζω . . . ἐπαιάζουσιν) and in its sense the eroticism of the verse: I wail for Adonis; the Loves wail too.

In the next stanza we have the first hint of the pathetic fallacy in this poem. His own hounds lament for the boy. The mountain nymphs weep too (18–19). This is, however, more like Achilles' horses weeping for the death of Patroclus.[2] Those horses were divine; it was not surprising that they could cry. Adonis' hounds are special too, in that they are his. That dogs, like Argos, should mourn for their master's death does not astound us either. In the following stanza, however, we have the pathetic fallacy full-blown. "Woe for Cypris, say all the hills, and all the oaks say, Woe for Cypris; the rivers weep for the sorrows of Aphrodite, and the mountain springs cry for Adonis;

---

1. Gow, *Theocritus* II, 54.
2. See J. L. Buller, "The Pathetic Fallacy in Hellenistic Pastoral," *Ramus* 10 (1981) 41.

the blossoms flush red for grief" (31–35). The theme of red and white that flows erotically through the poem occurs in another, implicit, instance of the pathetic fallacy. The red of Adonis' blood, the white of his flesh, are reflected in lines 64–66: "The Paphian sheds as many tears as Adonis does drops of blood, and on the ground both become blossoms—the blood brings to birth the rose, the tears the anemone." What lies behind this passage is the assumption that man and nature are intimately involved with one another.[3]

Later in the poem, the poet tells Aphrodite to cast garlands and flowers upon the corpse of Adonis as he lies on his golden couch. "As he died, so have all the blossoms withered too. Sprinkle him with Syrian ointments. Sprinkle him with myrrh. Let every perfume die; your perfume Adonis is dead" (76–78). This is the pathetic fallacy carried to a sensual, even morbid extreme.

Pseudo-Moschus' *Lament for Bion*, which is of course later than Bion's *Lament for Adonis*, is inspired by the earlier lament and by Thyrsis' song in Theocritus' *Idyll* I, and it combines aspects of each. Indeed, it might be said to be an exaggeration of each. The poet here mourns another, real-life poet, not an imaginary cowherd or a mythological lover of Venus, and virtually all of nature laments for him. "Cry me woe, glades and Dorian water, and weep, you rivers, for lovely Bion now mourn, you orchards, and now, you glades, give moan; breathe, blossoms, with clusters dishevelled; now, roses, redden your sorrows; now anemones, now hyacinths, tell your letters and in your petals take more the cry of woe. The beautiful musician is dead" (1–7). The ethical dative μοι "me" in line 3 is effective; it makes this lament more personal than its forebears. Pseudo-Moschus was presumably a pupil of Bion. Roses that literally redden their grief (φοινίσσεσθε τὰ πένθιμα 5) is a bold expression, quite modern in its proleptic quality. Next the nightingales and swans are bid tell that Bion, the Dorian Orpheus, is dead (14–18). The hills are dumb, and the cows that wander with the bulls make moan and are unwilling to pasture (23–24). The satyrs lament him and the black-robed Priapuses. Pans mourn his song, and throughout the woods the nymphs of the springs grieve and their waters become tears (27–29). This last is a pretty conceit, a reversal of the expected metamorphosis. In sorrow for Bion "the trees have cast their fruit and all the flowers have withered. The lovely milk flows not from the flocks, nor honey from the hives, for it has dried in the comb for grief—one can no longer gather it, now that that honey of yours is dead" (31–35). This is an extravagance of expression that goes beyond grief to conceit.

The pathetic fallacy implies that man and nature are somehow akin. This idea may have derived from Stoic philosophy, which saw all of creation as sharing in the same divine fire, but it seems far more likely to have come from what is a "primitive" belief, that mankind wields a sympathetic magic over nature. If man is sad, nature mourns. Toward the end of Pseudo-Moschus'

3. Ibid. 45–48.

epitaph for Bion, we have a corollary of the pathetic fallacy. Nature mourns for man because he alone dies once and for all: "Ah, the mallows, when in the garden they die and the fresh green parsley and the springing curl of the anise, they live again and grow for another year; but we, the mighty and strong, wise men, when once we die, we sleep unhearing in the hollow earth, well and long, a sleep that is unending and with no awakening" (99–104). It is man's mortality that makes him unique, a fit subject for grief.[4]

The pathetic fallacy, which in its pure form seems original to the Hellenistic period, is more difficult to document in art than it is in literature. The problem is complicated by the fact that we must rely upon Roman copies of Greek wall paintings, in which, significantly, the human figures may have been larger in proportion to the landscapes than they are in the copies. Still, even if they were considerably larger, they would probably have been relatively small in relation to the natural scenery that surrounded them.[5] This may seem to contradict the pathetic fallacy, in which man, in projecting his feelings upon nature seems to assume a man-centered universe, one in which he, by a sympathetic magic, controls nature. If, however, we look at these landscapes in art, we see that the implication is basically the same.

In the Abduction of Hylas, from which the figures of the nymphs and Hylas are now missing, we have a sky of threatening blue, a tree with spiky brown foliage and a trunk leaning dangerously to the left, a small altar and a white mass of rock to the right, all illuminated by an eerie, stormlike light. The whole landscape seems to cry aloud in horror at the deed (fig. 20). The original painting is thought to date to the second or first century B.C. The mood is far more romantic than that of the Hylas episode in either Apollonius of Rhodes (I.1223ff.) or Theocritus, *Idyll* XIII, which date to the third century B.C.

A landscape with figures similar in feeling to the Abduction of Hylas is that at Pompeii, probably from an original of the second century B.C., of a rocky landscape with a shrine and a man leading a ram to the altar. We have here too an eerie light and a setting with dreamlike rocks—green, rose, blue, lavender, and greenish-browns—that dwarf but also encompass and so set off the human and animal figures (fig. 76).

The controversial Odyssey frieze, which had been heavily restored and which may nor may not be a copy of a Greek original,[6] is our best evidence for the pathetic fallacy in art. In the scene of the attack of the Laestrygonians the landscape may dwarf the figures and so become, as Havelock has said, the

---

4. Ibid. 48.

5. R. Ling, "Hylas in Pompeian Art," *Mélanges d'Archéologie et d'Histoire de l'Ecole Française de Rome* 91 (1979) 787; P. H. von Blanckenhagen and C. Alexander, *The Paintings of Boscoreale* (Heidelberg, 1962) 50f. and n. 79.

6. On this subject see especially P. H. von Blanckenhagen, "The Odyssey Frieze," *Mitteilungen des deutschen archäologischen Instituts, Römische Abteilung* 70 (1963) 100–137.

76. Man with ram in rocky landscape, Museo Nazionale, Naples

painter's "romantic hero," but actually that landscape is in intimate sympathy with those figures (fig. 77).[7] Not only does the pool reflect the goat drinking from it—a naturalistic touch—but the trees of the landscape all twist and bend in harmony with and in opposition to the struggling human figures below them. The tree in the foreground, nearest the pool, which the Laestrygonian giant tries to pull down, bends with harmony of line to match the curve of his body, then twists back in opposition; finally, its splayed branches—like arms spread in desperation—seem to humanize the whole organism. This is more than realism. It is nature, huge as it is, bent to the whims of man. It is the pathetic fallacy.

7. Havelock, *HA* 264.

77. Attack of the Laestrygonians from the Odyssey Frieze, Vatican Museum

IX

The Creatures

The Hellenistic poets were, it is true, in some part antiquarians. The *Aitia* of both Callimachus and Apollonius attest to this. They were not, however, as so often claimed, just dry-as-dust scholars and librarians. They were inspired not only by the past, by the books in their libraries, but by the new developments in the Alexandrian science of their own day. One can point to a number of instances of this influence in their verse.

Callimachus, probably an associate of the physician Herophilus at the Mouseion, seems to show knowledge of Herophilus' work *On the Eyes*. In *Aitia* III, fr. 85, 15, he declares that Zeus Epopsois is unable to look at sinners with "cheerful eyes" (ἰθαροῖς λογάσιν). The word λογάδες means the whites or outer coat (scelera) of the eyes, and Fraser speculates that this rather grotesque detail is due to Callimachus' interest in Herophilus' work, even though that particular word is not recorded as having been used by Herophilus, who called the outer coat either χίτων λευκός or κερατοειδής. Still more suggestive is Callimachus' comparison of the Cyclops' eye in the *Hymn to Artemis* (III.53) to a shield of four oxhides (σάκει τετραβοείῳ) rather than to the usual Homeric σάκος ἑπταβόειον.[1] Oppermann considered this coinage to reflect Callimachus' knowledge of Herophilus' discovery of the four tunics of the eye.[2]

Apollonius of Rhodes seems also to reflect medical theory of his own day. When he describes Medea's passion for Jason, he says that the pain smoldered through her flesh and around her fine sinews (ἶνας III.763) and

1. Fraser, *Ptolemaic Alexandria* I, 356.
2. H. Oppermann, "Herophilos bei Kallimachos," *Hermes* 60 (1925) 16–32.

"as far down as the lowest part of the occipital bone of the head." This last is usually taken to be the nape of the neck, but the technical language is not just poetic variation. As Solmsen has pointed out, ἴνας must in this context be translated "nerves," and the play of this word with ἰνίον ("nape") certainly suggests that Apollonius for the moment reveals his knowledge of Herophilus' and Eristratus' discovery of the nerves. Indeed, Solmsen says in regard to this passage, "We might wish to ask: Did Herophilus or Eristratus think of the nerves as carriers not only of sense perceptions . . . but also of emotions? Had the seat of pain . . . been transferred from the heart to the brain? Does ἰνίον allude to a localization of the nerve-endings in the cerebellum?" [3]

In Book IV (1518–25) Apollonius again reveals medical knowledge. Not only is his description of Mopsus' death as the result of stepping upon a poisonous snake remarkable for its detailed account of his narcosis, but the word Apollonius uses for shin, κερκίς, literally "shuttle," was apparently first so used by Herophilus.[4] The word κάρος, used to describe Phineus' torpor in Book II (203), though it may have had a general use as "drowsiness," certainly had a technical medical use. Galen says that Hippocrates used it in reference to the disease of the temporal muscles.[5]

Apollonius seems to have used the work of an historian, Timaeus, for details, particularly ethnographical, of the Argonauts' return journey through central Europe and Italy; but a geographer, Timagetus, apparently contributed information for the Balkan stage of the journey, for Apollonius follows him in the mistaken hypothesis of a bifurcation of the Danube somewhere in the northern Balkans.[6]

Apollonius was not only familiar with the medical, historical, and geographical research of his day; he was also so well versed in astronomical lore that he constructed his epic in accordance with it.[7] The Argo, the Golden Fleece, the Eridanus, and the Lyre played by Orpheus are constellations. The Argonauts are either themselves constellations or the sons or grandsons of constellations. The Argonauts set sail before the ploughing season, that is, before the setting of the Pleiades in November, and Apollonius may have chosen a fall sailing date for his heroes because the "morning setting" of the constellation Argo was a calendar sign for autumn. Astronomical phenomena throughout are in accordance with other weather signs that establish a calendar for the voyage of the Argo. For instance, when the Argonauts were in Colchis in late spring, the constellation Orion was described as visible at sunset, as it

3. F. Solmsen, "Greek Philosophy and the Discovery of the Nerves," *Museum Helveticum* 18 (1969) 196.
4. Galen XIV.688.
5. Ibid. VIII.231.
6. Fraser, *Ptolemaic Alexandria* I, 626–27.
7. All the information in this paragraph is taken from P. Bogue's unpublished dissertation, "Astronomy in the *Argonautica* of Apollonius Rhodius" (Univ. of Illinois, Urbana, 1977).

in fact would have been from December to May. The Coronoa Borealis was shining all night, as it would have in April and May, and Ursa Major set at midnight, as it would actually have done about May 1. Even similes seem to have astronomical point. Jason, for instance, is described as rising like Sirius from the Ocean at the very hour that the star would in fact have risen from the Ocean. The voyage of the Argo, furthermore, seems in Apollonius' epic to reflect various aspects of the appearance—or nonappearance—of the constellation Argo in the sky. The ship Argo leaves Pagasae with her wake trailing behind her. Manilius took that description of her wake to refer to the Milky Way, upon which the constellation Argo floats. The ship Argo was invisible during the months when the constellation was invisible, and Apollonius described it as heading toward permanent destruction as it sailed toward the ocean north of Europe, where the constellation Argo is in fact never visible. Finally, when the ship Argo is swept, presumably by the Etesian winds at the rising of Sirius on July 28 or 29, to Africa, where the constellation appears to be borne aloft in the air, the ship is borne on men's shoulders or passed along by the hands of the Nereids.

The astronomical interpretation of the north frieze of the Great Altar of Zeus at Pergamum has for the most part been abandoned,[8] and I know of no other reflection in the visual arts of strictly astronomical lore, but other scientific interests of the Alexandrian age do make their appearance in painting, sculpture, and mosaics. The anatomical discoveries of Herophilus surely affected the sculptors of the exaggeratedly deformed skeletons of hunchbacks and the exaggerated musculature of the figures on the Pergamum frieze. The interest too in dwarfs and other deformed human beings which we see in mosaics and figurines may stem from the medical school in Alexandria. It is in the science of optics, however, that we see the most striking parallels between the literary and the visual arts.

Mirrors, so essential to a woman's toilet, are an element of the erotic in Hellenistic poetry. Callimachus in the *Bath of Pallas* tells the daughters of Achaea not to bring a mirror for Pallas, for not even at the judgment of Paris did she look into the orichale nor the waters of Simois—nor did Hera. "But Cypris took the shining bronze and often rearranged and again rearranged the same lock" (V.21–22). This is a charming vignette of feminine vanity, and the mention of the mirror is not at all surprising. In Book I of the *Argonautica* Cytherea appears on Jason's cloak "wrought with deep tresses and wielding Ares' swift shield. From her shoulder to her left arm the fastening of her tunic was loosed beneath her breast, and opposite in the brazen shield her image appeared just as she stood clear to see" (742–46). There is a hint here too of the sexuality and the fitting vanity of Aphrodite, but Apollonius' chief interest

8. For a summary of the scholarship on the frieze see Pollitt, *AHA* 105–9 and his bibliography, 296.

seems to be in the reflection of her in the shield. In the same century we
find similar subject matter in paintings. The Roman painting of Thetis in the
workshop of Hephaestus, which may be a copy of a third century B.C. original
by Theon of Samos, shows a properly diminished and reversed image of Thetis
in the convex surface of a bronze shield (fig. 12). In the Alexander Mosaic,
which may be a copy of an original of about 300 B.C., a Persian stares at his
own reflection, also diminished, in a polished shield (fig. 11). We are told too
that Sosus in his famous mosaic showed "a dove who is drinking and casts
the shadow of its head on the water" (Pliny, *NH* XXXVI.184). The care with
which the artists present the images suggests that they and Apollonius, who is
also precise (see above I.745: ἀτρεκὲς αὕτως "exactly so"), were aware of
Heron's and Pseudo-Euclid's work on catoptrics. Pseudo-Euclid may actually
have been Theon of Alexandria.[9]

Apollonius composed a strikingly original simile to describe Medea's
anxiety for Jason: "Her heart throbbed fast within her breast as when a beam
of the sun quivers inside the house as it leaps from water just poured into a
caldron or pail, and now here, now there, on the swift eddy it shimmers and
bounces along" (III.755–59). Apollonius' observation here may have been
sharpened by his awareness of Heron's and Euclid's work in optics, but it is
just as likely that he was inspired by the painters who were his contemporaries.
Greek optics was so entirely geometrical in method that its influence is likely
to have been indirect rather than direct, and Apollonius, as is clear throughout
his work, saw with a painter's eye and produced chiaroscuro effects very much
like theirs.[10]

Although one can point to specific instances of the effect of Alexandrian
science upon painters and poets alike, the deeper influence is one of attitude
and interest rather than specific subject matter or even technique. Artists are
interested in the particular, for it is through the particular that they express
the universal, but in the Hellenistic period both painters and poets show what
one might call a scientific, almost clinical interest in specificity, or what Hurst
called "le vérifiable."[11] A wonderful example of this is the famous Unswept
Floor mosaic of Sosus, the original of which would have dated to the early
second century B.C. (fig. 78). Here every object, from nutshell to mouse, is
enhanced by its shadow—another instance, perhaps, of the influence of the
science of optics.

The new exaggerated realism is evident in the figurines of dwarfs and
hunchbacks, in the large-scale sculptures of gods and giants in the Pergamum
frieze. It is also evident in the representations in both the literary and the visual
arts of animals. This representation varies in spirit from the naively realistic to

9. P. Ver Ecke, *Euclide, L'Optique et la Catoptrique* (Paris, 1959) xxix.
10. See below, Chapter 12.
11. A. Hurst, *Apollonius de Rhodes, manière et cohérence* (Rome, 1967) 12.

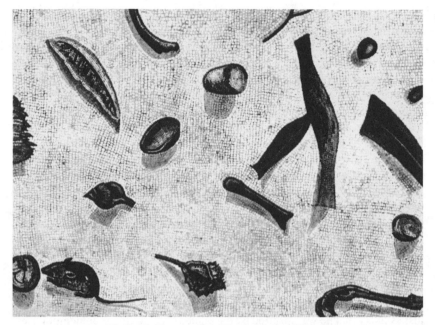

78. Detail, Unswept Floor Mosaic, Vatican Museum

the highly stylized, and elements other than the scientific enter in: the playful, the erotic, the pastoral, and the grotesque. Still, nothing is more revealing of the Hellenistic aesthetic than its artists' affection for the creatures.

The genre most strikingly original in the Hellenistic period is the pastoral. In Theocritus for the first time we encounter sheep and goats in a setting that is almost purely playful. Here too in *Idyll* I we have Daphnis bidding farewell to the wolves and jackals and bears in their mountain caves. These are a far cry from the lions, boars, horses, and hounds that we are accustomed to from archaic and classical literature and art. The pastoral mode does not, however, appear in the visual arts until late in the Hellenistic period and then in Roman painting. A painting of about 25 B.C. from the Villa Pamphili in Rome presents a bucolic, probably African setting (fig. 79). In the center is a straw-built hut, with a stork on its roof. At either side of the painting is a rather impressionistically rendered tree. A man with a staff leans against the one at the right, and a seated dog turns its head to look back at him. Three cows graze to center and left. The mood is more truly rustic than almost anything else we have left to us from antiquity. The treatment too is both more realistic and more romantic than anything in Theocritus. We have here, in fact, almost left antiquity behind us.

Aratus, more obviously than any other Hellenistic poet, shows a scientific

79. African pastoral scene from the Villa Pamphili, Museo Nazionale, Rome

interest in animals. He, of course, follows self-consciously in the Hesiodic, didactic tradition. A part of his didacticism is his versification of the works of Eudoxus and Theophrastus. Governing it all perhaps is his Stoicism. The pattern in the skies is perpetuated in the patterns on earth. The same fire that shines through the stars appears in the souls of animals and men. This basic Stoic principle may account for his anthropomorphizing of Zeus' creatures. It is also what, almost accidentally, gives his Weather Signs such ingenuous charm.

Aratus may have versified the work of Theophrastus, but the detail that gives his work the specificity that is its charm is his own. "When oxen," he tells us, "lick around the hooves of their feet that are beneath the shoulders (i.e., their forefeet) or on their beds stretch themselves on their right sides, the old ploughman expects a delay of ploughing" (1114–17). What Theophrastus (15) says is "an ox licking its forehoof signifies storm or rain." Aratus writes "licking around," and his expression for forefoot, ὑπωμαίοιο, is certainly more vivid—if in fact it is not his own coinage—than Theophrastus' προσθίαν. Again, Aratus writes, "Nor when full of lowing the kine gather together coming stallward at the ox-loosing hour, do the heifers, sullen of the meadow and pasture, give notice that straightway they are going, stormless, to fill themselves" (1118–21). The middle form ἀγέρωνται "gather together" gives a vivid and realistic picture of what cattle actually do before a storm. The startling genitives λειμῶνος "meadow" and βουθοσίοιο "pasture," [12] with σκυθραί "sullen," are poetic invention, awkward perhaps but effective. Cows before a storm will eat for the next day. There is no model in Theophrastus for this passage. "Neither are goats," Aratus continues, "in fair weather eager for the holm-oak with its thorns, nor do sows rage furiously over their bedding" (1122–23). This last has a model in Theophrastus (49), who states that a com-

12. If that is indeed the construction. J. Martin, *Arati Phaenomena* (Florence, 1956) 150 on line 1120, writes: "Tout le monde accepte sans broncher la construction étonnant de σκυθραί avec deux génitifs: 'Regrettant avec tristesse le pré et la pâture.' Il y a pourtant au vers suivant un mot auquel les deux génitifs se rattacheraient avec infiniment plus de naturel: ἐμπλήσεσθαι." There is also the possibility that they are simply genitives of place.

80. Nilotic mosaic, House of the Faun, Pompeii

mon sign of stormy weather is "when sows fight over (μάχωνται) and carry (φέρωσιν) their bedding." Aratus writes μαργαίνουσαι, a Homeric word (*Il.* V.882). His sows achieve the status of Iliadic warriors. He follows perhaps but intensifies the statement of Democritus, who is reported by Plutarch (*Map.* 129a) to have said that a sign of rain was sows raging (μαργαινούσαις) over their bedding.

"When the lonely wolf howls loud, or when taking little heed of farmers, he comes down to ploughed fields of men, like one craving shelter, in order to find a lair there, when the third dawn comes round, expect a storm" (1124–28). That Aratus calls the wolf λύκος μονόλυκος gives pathos to the picture. His model Theophrastus (46) writes simply λύκος, and says only that the howling wolf signals a storm within three days' time and that his approach to the ploughed fields also indicates a storm. He says nothing of his being heedless of men or of his craving shelter. It is Aratus who humanizes him.

"Squeaking and dancing mice," says Theophrastus (41), "are a sign of storm." Here too Aratus embroiders a bit. "Nor were mice, if ever they squeaked more than was their wont in fair weather and skipped like dancers, unmarked by men of old" (1132–34). The verb he so colorfully adds is ἐσκίρτησαν "skipped."

"The dog rooting with its feet," says Theophrastus (42), "is a sign of storm." "The dog," says Aratus, "roots with both its feet, expecting that a storm is coming, and those mice too then prophesy a storm [and from the sea the crab makes its way landward when the storm is about to break, and in the daytime the mice tossing straw with their feet (ποσσὶ στιβάδα στρωφῶντες) are desirous (ἱμείρονται) of a bed, when signs of rain appear]" (1135–41). This last delightful detail about the prophetic mice appears to be Aratus' own.

The detailed observation and the charming naivete of the often awkward language of Aratus' poem does not find its parallel in the visual arts until a century or so later. Then, in a number of mosaics we find the same passion for "le vérifiable" that we see in the *Phaenomena*. Perhaps the work nearest in spirit to Aratus is the Nilotic mosaic from the House of the Faun at Pompeii (fig. 80). Here are the creatures and plants of the Delta's marshland, done in colorful detail, but set separately and like jeweled toys on a striated and sparkling water that does not seem really to recede into space. Everything is seen at equally close range. It is this together with the very specificity of rendering which gives this scene the somewhat primitive charm of Aratus' Weather Signs. One sees the very seed pods and stamens of plants, the teeth of the hippopotamus, the forked tongue of the snake, the webbed toes of the frog, not to mention the many marvelous shades of the marsh birds' plumage. The mosaic technique in itself lends to the whole a glitter that helps to create a sense of "magic realism" which goes beyond what Aratus has achieved.

81. Marine-life mosaic, House of the Faun, Pompeii

Two mosaics from Pompeii, both of which are probably copies of a Hellenistic original of the late second century B.C., show an exquisitely detailed and realistic depiction of marine life. In one of them the marine creatures fill the sky as well as the sea (fig. 81). Although the expression on all the creatures is perfectly fishlike, one does read into the various faces surprise, melancholy, disdain, suspicion, amusement, curiosity, concern. The treatment is in a subtle way anthropomorphic. The whole is just slightly humorous. But, as in the Nilotic mosaic, the chief concern is "le vérifiable."

Apollonius treats animals chiefly in similes, and these are for the most part Homeric in spirit and in the animals with which they deal: lions, ants, flies, bees, hawks, boars. One simile which displays a new realism, comparable to that of Aratus, occurs in Book II. The Argonauts drag their oars through the sea "even as ploughing oxen cleaving the moist earth toil, and unspeakable

82. Nilotic mosaic at Praeneste, Palestrina Archaeological Museum

sweat trickles from flanks and neck, and their eyes roll askance from beneath the yoke, and their parched breath roars incessantly from their mouths, and pressing their hooves in the earth, they toil all day" (662–67).[13]

Others have observed that the Nilotic mosaic at Praeneste exemplifies aspects of the Hellenistic aesthetic (fig. 82). Villard finds in it "a genuine synthesis of all the elements which go to make up the Alexandrian landscape with its inextricable blend of realistic observation and *genre* scenes which are distinctly artificial." [14] Hurst cites it as an example of "le vérifiable," noting that not only are the creatures in it represented with the most realistic detail but that they are actually named. He observes too that the intellect dominates this fecund display of nature: the waters of the Nile unite the varieties of

13. One thinks of Isak Dinesen's description of her oxen in *Out of Africa*: "They have been inspanned before daybreak, and have sweated up and down the long hills, and across dungas and river beds, through the burning hours of the day. . . . The bull is in a constant stage of fury, rolling his eyes, shovelling up the earth, upset by everything that gets within his range of vision, —still he has got a life of his own, fire comes from his nostrils, and new life from his loins; his days are filled with his vital cravings and satisfactions" ([New York, 1937; rep. 1972] 263).

14. F. Villard, "Painting," in Charbonneaux 176–77; Pollitt, *AHA* 205.

animal, vegetable, human, and architectural detail.[15] I should go further and say that this astounding mosaic, though it dates almost two centuries later—it was probably made by Greek artists on Italian soil at about 80 B.C.[16]—reflects or shares in the same aesthetic that governs Apollonius' epic.

A common complaint about the *Argonautica* is that it is episodic. It is, of course, that, but that is just exactly its organizing principle, for if one reads the epic straight through, one comes away from it with a most wonderful sense of voyage. The Argonauts visit one exotic people or landscape after another, and these encounters and adventures are all linked together by the course of the ship through the waters of the Aegean, the Mediterranean, the Propontis, the Ister, the Adriatic, the Eridanus, the Rhone, the Ionian, the Syrtes, and the Tritonian Lake. As Apollonius used the work of geographers, mistaken or not, to plot the course of the Argonauts, so the artists of the Praeneste mosaic attempted in the one-dimensional surface available to them to show the flow of the Nile and the varying degrees of civilization and wilderness that border it in its course.[17] At the bottom—that is, in the foreground—is Hellenized Egypt. Here we see colonnaded temples, Greek galleys, hoplites, and picnicking men and women in Greek clothing. Beyond that we see the brick pylons and osier huts of Egypt itself. In the waters are fishermen of a native cast of countenance, color, and dress in papyrus boats. The river itself teems with many varieties of plants, birds, and animals—ducks, ibises, storks, fish, hippopotami—and on islands we see crocodiles, oxen, and more hippopotami. Finally, the Nile brings us to savage desert country with its black Nubian hunters and still more exotic beasts—a rhinoceros, a wild boar, jackals, monkeys, a huge coiled snake, and storks and ibises in the air. The interest in plant and animal life is a reflection of the new science. There was probably in the time of the Ptolemies a zoo in Alexandria,[18] and Ptolemy II Philadelphus himself was responsible for the Grand Procession, which included a great variety of exotic animals. The text of Athenaeus' *Deipnosophists*, Book V, quoting from a longer work, *About Alexandria* by Callixeinos of Rhodes, lists elephants, saiga antelopes, oryxes, hartebeest, ostriches, onelaphoi, onagers, camels, and Indian, Hyrcanian, and Molossian hounds, as well as "one hundred and thirty Ethiopian, three hundred Arabian, and twenty Euboean sheep, twenty-six all-white Indian cows plus twenty Ethiopian ones, one large white bear, fourteen leopards, sixteen cheetahs, four caracels, three cheetah cubs, one giraffe, and

15. Hurst, *Apollonius de Rhodes* 12.

16. Villard, "Painting," in Charbonneaux 177. The mosaic is heavily restored.

17. For further illustrations of this mosaic see Charbonneaux, figs. 181–86.

18. Fraser, *Ptolemaic Alexandria* I, 5, 515; II, 743 n. 181. K. Phillips, "The Barberini Mosaic" (diss. Princeton, 1962) ii, says that the animals of the mosaic were inspired by an illustrated exploration account done for Ptolemy II and that many of these creatures had not been seen outside of Alexandria when the mosaic was constructed.

one Ethiopian rhinoceros." There were also "borne along in cages parrots, peacocks, guinea fowl, pheasants, and Ethiopian birds, many in number." [19] The loving detail, down to the very teeth, with which the exotic creatures of the Praeneste mosaic are rendered is an aspect of the Hellenistic aesthetic. The striated presentation of water and sky; the patches of light which pick out buildings, pieces of landscapes, the clothing of certain of the Greek figures, and even the rump of a hippopotamus, the face of the grinning rhinoceros; the shadows and reflections in the water—all are a part of the chiaroscuro which is so typical of Apollonius. Both he and the artists of the mosaic have illuminated "le vérifiable". Alexandrian science may have inspired them, but they imbued that science with magic.

Another voyage depicted in Hellenistic art is that of Telephus on the smaller frieze of the Great Altar of Zeus at Pergamum. It dates to the middle of the second century B.C. [20] and exemplifies another major achievement of the Hellenistic period: the presentation of continuous narrative in the pictorial arts. Here the entire tale of Telephus, a legendary ancestor of the Attalid monarchs, is told from birth to death in episodic fashion. The story was that Aleos, king of Arcadia, warned that his daughter Auge's sons would kill his own sons, put her to sea in a raft and had Telephus, her son by Heracles, exposed on a mountain side. Auge's raft drifted to Mysia, where she was befriended by King Teuthras. Telephus meanwhile was suckled by a lioness, discovered by Heracles, and brought up by a neighboring king. When he grew up, he slew Aleos' sons, found Auge, helped Teuthras in warfare, was rewarded by the promise of a marriage to Auge, fortunately forestalled by a serpent sent by Athene, which arranged a recognition between mother and son. Telephus became king of Mysia and fought in the Trojan War, where he was entangled in a vine of Dionysus and so wounded by Achilles. To heal his wound he journeyed to Argos to seek rust from the sword which had struck him. This he acquired only by holding Orestes hostage. He returned to Mysia, founded Pergamum, and established the Attalid dynasty.

On the remains of the frieze the hero himself appears more than once, first as an infant suckled by a lioness (fig. 83), then with his companions in Mysia (fig. 84), and still again seated in a palace in Argos and showing his wound to a Greek prince (fig. 85). This technique is in striking contrast to the archaic and classical narrative method, where several episodes, separate in time, are often condensed, symbolically, in a single picture. In the Telephus frieze we see first the building of the raft in which King Aleos put his daughter Auge to sea (fig. 86). Four workers, tools in hand, tilt the boat, realistically foreshortened, to construct it. Above them, to suggest a hillside, and on a smaller scale,

19. Rice, *The Grand Procession of Ptolemy Philadelphus* 16–21.
20. Pollitt, *AHA* 198.

83. Telephus suckled by a lioness, Staatliches Museum, East Berlin

to indicate distance, are three seated female figures. The veiled and grieving woman is probably Auge herself. Other panels show landscapes with rocks and trees and interiors with furniture, columns, and altars to indicate changes of scene as the narrative progresses. In its episodic nature this frieze is even more comparable to the *Argonautica* than the Praeneste mosaic.

The naivete of the animals in the Praeneste mosaic may result more from the ineptitude of the artists than from intent, but there is in the Hellenistic period an ingenuous depiction of animals, especially pets, that seems to be deliberate. This trend begins in literature early. Anyte, Mnasalces, and Nicias in the third century B.C. wrote epigrams for deceased pets that have an intentionally childlike charm, and they were successfully imitated by later epi-

84. Telephus with his companions in Mysia, Staatliches Museum,
East Berlin

grammatists. The *Anthology* brims with these delightful epitaphs for dolphins,
cocks, locusts, cicadas, ants, dogs, horses, and even a hare.

"For her locust, nightingale of the fields," writes Anyte (XX; *AP* 7.190),
"and her cicada that slept under the oak, Myrto fashioned a common tomb,
shedding a little girl's tear, for inexorable Hades had carried off her two pets."
Mnasalces (XII; *AP* 7.192) writes with similar simplicity: "No longer with
your shrill-voiced wings will you sing, locust, sitting in the fruited furrows,
nor will you delight me as I lie in the leafy shade, striking a sweet tune from
your tawny wings." Nicias (*AP* 7.200) writes what is presumably an epitaph
for a captured and probably killed grasshopper: "No longer, curled beneath
the leafy twig, will I delight in casting my voice from my delicate wings, for I
fell into the accursed hands of a boy who stealthily grasped me as I sat on the
green leaves." All of these are short statements, made without elaboration,

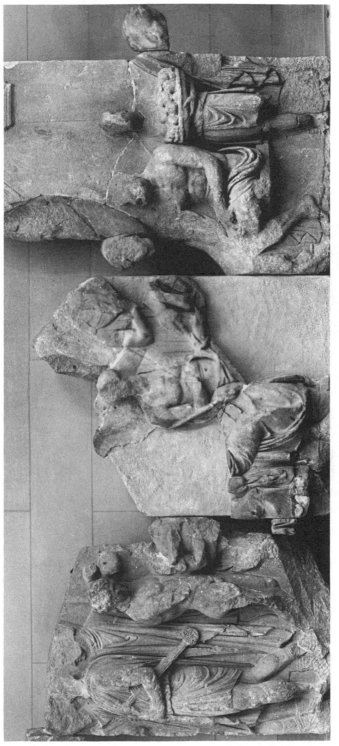

85. Telephus seated at banquet in Argos, Staatliches Museum, East Berlin

125

86. Building of the raft from the Telephus frieze, Staatliches Museum, East Berlin

description, or sentiment. They seem appropriate to a world of children and their pets. Anyte has too an epigram (XIII; *AP* 6.312), written perhaps as an inscription for a picture or relief, on children playing with a goat: "The children, billy-goat, have put crimson reins on you and a muzzle on your shaggy face. They play at horses with you around the temple of the god that he may see them in their childish joy." The brevity is again suggestive of the simplicity of childhood.

The spirit of childhood in the visual arts was nowhere more successfully evoked than by the rococo sculptures of the third century B.C. Two chubby little boys, scarcely more than infants, in a terra-cotta group at the Walters Art Gallery in Baltimore, watch the outcome of a cock fight (fig. 9). The champion of the winner smiles delightedly; the other leans his head on his arm in solemn but childlike resignation. A little girl, whose head is now missing, stands between. The victorious cock wears a severe, almost mean, expression;

the other is quite woebegone. They are rendered almost as humanly as the boys. The group is presented with more detail than are the epigrams of Anyte, Nicias, or Mnasalces, but the spirit of childhood and play is much the same. Other figures from this period display the same affection for both children and their pets. Perhaps the most ingenuous of these is the now headless little girl at the Metropolitan, New York, who holds a pet in the pouch of her dress; her charm is quite equal to that of Anyte's epigrams (fig. 33).

The Hellenistic epigrammatists specialized in little animals, but they wrote epitaphs for larger creatures too. Anyte has epitaphs on a war-horse (IX; *AP* 7.208) and a dolphin (XII; *AP* 7.215), and Tymnes (V; *AP* 7.211), perhaps also of the third century B.C., has an effective epitaph for a dog: "The stone says that it holds here the white dog of Melite, Eumelos' most faithful guard. They called him Bull when he lived, but now the quiet paths of night contain his voice." This may have been a small lap dog, or a dog represented on vases as Μελιταῖος which is "medium-sized, wooly-coated, and curly-tailed." [21] If so, the epithet ταῦρος would be a kind of joke, an affectionate name for a small but fierce watchdog. On the other hand, the dog may have been called that because of his massive stature, or because of a deep voice. We have late in the Hellenistic period realistic portrayals of both kinds of dogs: the powerful bull mastiff in the Vatican (fig. 87); the small pet dog curled up on a couch in the Altes Museum, Berlin (fig. 88). We have in these sculptures two extremes of the Hellenistic perception: suprarealism in the case of the former to portray the power of the beast; a coy mannerism in the case of the latter to show the creature's sweet appeal. Neither preserves the simple realism of Anyte and her followers or the naive naturalism of Aratus and the mosaicists.

Alongside this trend toward realism ran another. There was throughout the Hellenistic period a tendency to use animals in both literature and art as decorative elements. The treatment was sometimes precious, sometimes manneristic, and often very elegant. One sees the beginning of it in Callimachus. In the *Hymn to Artemis* the poet tells us that Pan gave to Artemis "two dogs, black and white, three reddish, one spotted;" he also gave her "seven Cynosurian bitches swifter than the winds, the swiftest to pursue fawns and the hare which never closes its eyes, swiftest too to mark the lair of the deer and where the burrow of the porcupine is, and to lead upon the track of the gazelle" (III.93–97). The lists here—the colors of the dogs, the prey of the hounds— seem to be added for decorative effect. They are meant to charm, and they do. They are comparable to the animal and floral borders that we see in the mosaics of the Hellenistic period (e.g., fig. 81).

An Alexandrian touch in the *Hymn to Demeter* is the list of the things that Erysicthon ate: "He ate the mules that they loosed from the great wagons;

---

21. A.S.F. Gow and D. L. Page, *The Greek Anthology: Hellenistic Epigrams* II (Cambridge, 1965) 555.

87. Bull mastiff, Vatican Museum

he ate the heifer that his mother was fattening for Hera; he ate the race horse and the war-horse; and he ate the cat at which the vermin trembled (τὰν ἔτρεμε θηρία μικκά)" (VI.107–110). The whole sequence is funny, and the final item, with its attention to the tiny vermin, is amusing in a particularly Alexandrian manner. These artists took delight in what was small, everyday, and hitherto neglected in art. One thinks of the mouse in the Unswept Floor mosaic.

In one of his *Aitia* (fr. 177), *The Mousetrap*, Callimachus presents a delightful description of mice at their mischief: "Often they licked the fat oil from the lamps, drawing it off with their tails, when the lid was not on it . . . they danced on his head and drove sleep away from the corners of his eyes. . . . But this was the most shameless thing that the thieves accom-

88. Dog on couch, Staatliches Museum, East Berlin

plished in the short night. . . . The rogues gnawed through his clothes and his goat's-hair cloak and his wallet." In something of the same vein Leonidas of Tarentum (XXXVII; *AP* 6.302), an approximate contemporary of Callimachus, addresses the σκότιοι μύες—mice that love the dark—and tells them that he cannot afford to feed them; he is content if he has salt and two barley cakes. It is again the mood of the Unswept Floor (fig. 78). No creature is too small, too commonplace, for the artist's attention.

Leonidas' treatment of the mice is a bit more precious than that of Callimachus. So too is his epitaph for a locust (XXI; *AP* 7.198) more elaborate, more decorative than that of Anyte for Myrto's pets. In his the locust itself speaks. Addressing the passerby, it says: "Though the tombstone on my grave seems small, do not reproach Philainis. Her singing locust that walked on thistles, that looked like a straw, she loved and cherished for two years, because I made a melodious sound. And not even when I'd died did she cast me away but made me this little tomb for my many-strophied song." The details—that he walked on thistles, looked like a straw—and the emphasis on smallness —μικρός, line 1, τὠλίγον, line 8—are charmingly Alexandrian.

We see the same lightness of touch in Callimachus' *Aitia* I, "Against the Telchines," when he speaks of himself as a poet of the new breed. "We sing," he says, "among those [who love?] the shrill voice of the cicadas . . . and not the noise of the asses. Let another bray like the long-eared beast; may I be the dainty (οὐλ[α]χύς), the winged one . . . that I sing living on dew, ready sustenance from the divine air" (29–34). He is of course referring to his technique as a poet, but the delicacy of his art is comparable to the delicacy we see in the representation of animals in the visual arts all through the Hellenistic period.

89. Mule protome, Metropolitan Museum of Art, New York.

The bronze protome of a mule in the Metropolitan Museum, New York, which dates probably to the late second or early first century B.C., is more slender and more elegant than ever any mule was (fig. 89). The curve of its neck, the angle of its ears, the look askance of its eyes, which were inlaid with silver, the irregular tufts of its mane, give the animal the liveliness of a dancer, while the soft, elongated muzzle is almost sentimental in its effect. The whole is both more and less than realistic. The skinny greyhound gnawing at a bone (fig. 90), also in the Metropolitan, and the pair of playing hounds at the Vatican Museum (fig. 91) have the same lightness of touch, but while both are humorous in treatment, the playing hounds are almost ballerina-like in their slender grace.

90. Greyhound with bone, Metropolitan Museum of Art, New York

91. Playing hounds, Vatican Museum

The most delicate treatment of creatures comes in the silver and gold work of the Hellenistic period. Animals and birds are of course favorite decorative motifs the world over. Their intrinsic beauty and their otherness account for this. In Greek art of the Mycenaean and Archaic periods the frequent appearance of animal motifs can be attributed, in part at least, to "orientalizing." In the Hellenistic period it can be attributed, again at least in part, to Alexander's conquests. The appearance of certain exotic animals is probably due to Persian, even Indian influence. This is particularly true of gold jewelry, where we

92. Necklace with elephant-head terminals, private collection

find many bracelet, collar, and necklace terminals of lynx, antelope, gazelle, and lion heads. The Indian influence is seen in a unique pair of bejewelled elephant heads of elaborately chased gold which serve as the terminals of a garnet, rock crystal, and emerald necklace (fig. 92). At one time the elephants wore wreaths studded with small stones or possibly pearls. Their curled trunks are made of thick pieces of gold with horizontal notches. Hoffman speculates that the meaning of the piece is Dionysiac, "relating to the god's triumph." [22] The necklace, which is in a private Swiss collection, dates to the third century B.C.

From northern Greece in the second half of the third century B.C. we have an even more elaborate creation. It is a gold pin crowned by a Corinthian capital, surmounted by a dove, whose feathers are made of small loops of rope-wire filigree (fig. 93).[23] The loops may once have contained light blue and green glass. The dove's eyes are made of a dark red glass and simply fused to the gold. Another larger piece of red glass is set in the center of each wing. The bird wears a gold-rosette crown and a complicated harness. On his breast he has four small rosettes set in the partitions made by the harness. He is even more than Callimachean in his elaborate elegance.

22. Hoffman and Davidson, *Greek Gold* 188 and pl. V.
23. Ibid. 131 and fig. 45b.

93. Dove pin, private collection

The piece of jewelry that is perhaps most like Callimachus' cicada living on dew is a butterfly pendant from Olbia in southern Russia, now in a private collection, which dates to the late third or early second century B.C. (fig. 94). The creature's head is a heart-shaped garnet; its thorax, another, oval-shaped garnet; its abdomen is an elongated brown sardonyx bead with a white horizontal stripe. At the end of the abdomen are three graduated gold granules. The wings are outlined with beaded gold wire and divided by gold cloisons into sections filled with dark and light blue and light green enamel. The legs and antennae are made of plain scrolled wire. At the ends are knobbed pins which may once have contained pearls. For delicacy and elegance nothing can surpass this exquisite pendant.

The decorative elegance of the Hellenistic period is combined with its accurate observation of creatures in a silver cosmetic box, reported to be from

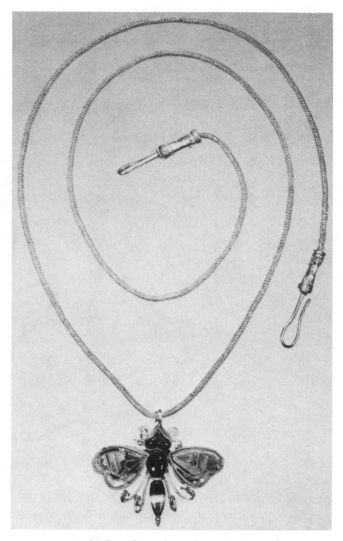

94. Butterfly pendant, private collection

Paterno, Sicily, and dated to the third century B.C. (fig. 95). It is a stylized but life-size rendering of a scallop shell. On the cover is an equally stylized octopus, as beautiful as a dancer, the coils of its arms and of the "veins" of its body contrasting most effectively with the rayed ridges of the scallop's shell. The silversmith, like the makers of the marine mosaics, knew his biology. Aristotle (*Historia Animalium* 519.a.1) remarks that the octopus feeds on shell-fish. Finally, the toggle pin that holds the hinge is in the shape of a serpent.

95. Scallop-shell cosmetic box,
Antikenmuseum, West Berlin

Later in the Hellenistic period we have a more precious treatment of animals. Meleager writes of all the usual small creatures: grasshoppers, butterflies, mosquitoes, bees. An epitaph on a hare is a particularly good example of his sentimentality and wit (LXV; *AP* 7.207). The creature himself speaks: "Phanion of the delicious flesh fed and cherished me in her bosom, a swift-footed, long-eared leveret, torn from my mother's breast while yet a babe, and fed me on flowers of spring. No more did I long for my mother, but I died of a surfeit of food, fattened by many a banquet. She buried my corpse next to her bed so that in her dreams she might see my bed beside her couch." The sensuousness of ἐν κόλποις "in her bosom" and γλυκερόχρως, literally "sweet-skinned" or "sweet-fleshed," contrasts delightfully with the humor of the little rabbit's having eaten himself to death. His grave beside his mistress's bed is the final and sentimental touch.

Meleager has epigrams, amatory rather than funereal, even though both are included in *AP* VII, on a locust and a cicada, which are more detailed in their descriptions of the insects than are those of his predecessors. They are also more sentimental in their content. In the first (XII; *AP.* 7.195) he asks the locust to play him a tune beating with his dear feet his talking wings (ἐγκρούουσα φίλοις ποσσὶ λάλους πτέρυγας 4), so that he may sleep and for a time be free of the care of love. In the morning, he promises him, he will give him a fresh green leek and drops of dew sprayed from his mouth. The second (XIII; *AP.* 7.196) is in much the same vein. Here the poet asks the noisy cicada to shrill with his sawlike legs against his sunburnt skin a tune of the lyre (πριονώδεσι κώλοις / αἰθίοπι κλάζεις χρωτὶ μέλισμα λύρας 3–4). This musical skill is perhaps reflected in the precious grasshoppers, emblems from a pair of dishes, reported to be from Nihawand, Iran, and

96. Grasshopper medallions, Staatliche Antikensammlungen und Glyptothek, Munich

dating to the second century B.C. (fig. 96). They are modelled of silver in high relief. Their hind legs are undercut. Their anatomy is treated in accurate but stylized detail. Their faces, as they chew on the also stylized grapevines on which they are perched, are both buglike and humanized. They are certainly expressive of something—if of nothing else, of the earnestness of eating. The most amusing and Meleager-like aspect of these creatures is that their forelegs are made of separate pieces of wire that pass through and to the backs of the reliefs and can be made to move. It is this attention to the peculiar detail that is the charm of the late Hellenistic period. It is childlike, pretty, witty, and sometimes piquant.

X

Eroticism

One of the most charming features of the Hellenistic aesthetic is the subtle eroticism that pervades both the poetry and the visual arts. This differs from the romantic passion of Medea for Jason. It touches the senses rather than the emotions; it delights rather than disturbs.

It is of course a commonplace to say that it was the Hellenistic age that discovered the nude female form, and indeed we have from this period a number of nude figures, especially, and fittingly, of Aphrodite. Perhaps the most sensuous of all is the Crouching Aphrodite. One of many Roman copies is housed in the Museo Nazionale delle Terme in Rome (fig. 97). The original, usually attributed to Doidalsas, dated to 250–240 B.C. and was probably of bronze. The torsion of the body, a major achievement of the Hellenistic artist, as well as the crouching position result in realistic folds of flesh from just below the breasts to the lower belly. The breasts themselves point outward and from their sheer fullness fall slightly downward, again in a realistic manner that is remarkably sensuous. The erotic quality of the statue is enhanced by the position of the legs which just conceal the pudenda and, before they were lost, by the arms, which were modestly crossed in front of the body. The face, with its heavy-lidded eyes and full, parted lips, is highly individualized. This Aphrodite seems not so much a goddess as a perfectly recognizable, sweet, and yet sensuous young woman.

Female flesh in all its beauty was a major achievement of the Hellenistic sculptors. It occurred later too, as we have seen, in the painters. The painting of the Three Graces, based on a sculptured group of the first century B.C., shows the rosy quality of the flesh that the sculptors can only suggest (fig. 18). Callimachus in *Hymn* V, *The Bath of Pallas*, suggests both the flesh and its

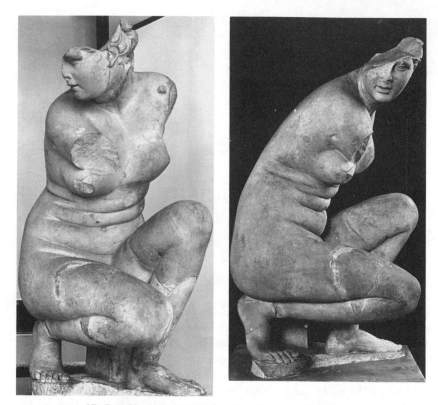

97. Crouching Aphrodite, Museo Nazionale delle Terme, Rome

color when he says that the goddess anointed herself (ἐτρίψατο 25) with simple unguents, and the blush ran up her (τὸ δ' ἔρευθος ἀνέδραμε 27) like the red (κόκκος 28) of the morning rose or the seed of the pomegranate. The verbs ἀνέδραμε and ἐτρίψατο (in the middle) both suggest the third dimension of the flesh and the mention of the rose its color. The bath here, as it is in sculpture, is of religious significance. Its portrayal is, however, erotic, which is of course appropriate also to Doidalsas' Aphrodite.

The delicate eroticism which appears in the Crouching Aphrodite and in Callimachus' description of Athene anointing herself is reflected even in the minor arts of the third century B.C. A silver cosmetic box, reported to be from Asia Minor, has a lid which is shaped and decorated, probably deliberately, to resemble the female breast (fig. 98). It is of plain, subtly swelling silver but has in its center a gilded rosette and surrounding patterns which are molded to suggest a nipple. Again, the eroticism is delicate and totally charming.

Less subtle perhaps but equally appealing is a gold medallion, probably a breast ornament, which shows a winged Eros as a plump and extremely

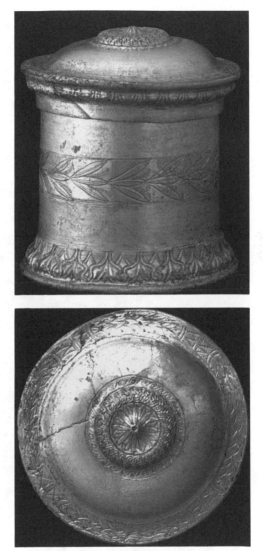

98. Silver cosmetic box, Museum of
Fine Arts, Boston

sensuous child in bacchanalian attire: grape leaves, ivy, and berries in his
hair; clusters of grapes over his ears; a fawn skin over his shoulder; a torque
with animal heads around his neck; and a serpentine armlet on his right arm
(fig. 99). His bust protrudes from the ornament in a manner which in itself
suggests a breast and nipple, and his profile with its full, protruding lips and
faintly near-eastern nose, the swell of his throat, and the heavy lids of his eyes
exude an eroticism that surpasses even that of the front view, where his plump
cheeks and shoulders are as sensuous as all that he himself and his costume

99. Breast ornament with Eros, Louvre, Paris

stand for. This medallion is perhaps Syrian and dates to the late fourth or early third century B.C.

By contrast, Apollonius' Eros in Book III of the *Argonautica* is quite an innocent fellow—although he apparently is clever enough to cheat at dice. When his mother finds him, he is holding the palm of his left hand quite full of them under his breast (ὑπὸ μαζῷ 119), but on the flesh of his cheek a sweet blush blossoms (γλυκερὸν δέ οἱ ἀμφὶ παρειάς / χροιῆς θάλλεν ἔρευθος 121–22). There is, after all, a hint here of the erotic. There is perhaps also that in the scene which follows Aphrodite's promise of Zeus' ball to the child. "He threw down all his toys, and catching with both hands, now on this side, now on that, at her robe, clung passionately to the goddess. She turned and spoke to him and drew him toward her" (146–50). In art Aphrodite is often presented together with Eros. In some versions of the Crouching Aphrodite he is in fact thought to have held a mirror for her. Mirrors are generally associated with the erotic. A third-century B.C. gold, garnet, and glass medallion, said to be from Pagasae, Thessaly, has a protruding bust of Aphrodite with a small winged Eros over her left shoulder (fig. 100). This ornament may have been attached to a hair net—a piece of female adornment. The sexuality of childhood is conversely suggested by Aphrodite herself in another piece of gold jewelry, possibly from Alexandria, which also dates to the third century B.C. (fig. 101). The goddess forms the finial of a pin. She stands, her left hip thrust to one side, only her legs covered by her drapery, and carries a small Eros, who leans over her left shoulder. The shortened proportions of her body are somehow childlike, which makes the contrasting fullness of breasts and hip all the more suggestive. She is one of the most erotic of all Aphrodites, and her sexuality resides precisely in her childlike proportions.

There are innumerable winged Erotes dangling from gold earrings of the Hellenistic period. Sometimes Eros is masked. Often he plays a musical instrument; often too, he emerges from the calyx of a flower. The last two motifs are combined in a gold applique from Palaiokastron: a plump baby plays a flute in the calyx of an acanthus.[1] In an elaborate set of earrings from Kyme in Asia Minor which date to the second half of the fourth century B.C. we find, in the Hellenistic spirit, winged Erotes suspended on chains playing with the *iynx* or magic wheel (fig. 102). From the upper disc are suspended figures of dolls. It has been conjectured that these earrings were part of a girl's nuptial attire. The Greek bride, who might be only thirteen or fourteen years old, often dedicated her dolls to Aphrodite on the eve of her wedding.[2] Another pair of gold earrings from Kalymnos, similar in style and dating to the same period, have crouching Nikes, Eros' female counterparts, holding dice; from their spreading wings, which are fastened to the back of the upper disc by loops, there are suspended on chains two figures of veiled dancers and two dolls (fig. 103). The two sets of earrings were presumably for similar functions. They represent the elements of magic and chance in affairs of the heart as well as the bride's dedication to Aphrodite.[3]

1. Hoffman and Davidson, *Greek Gold*, fig. 131.
2. R. Zahn, *Ausstellung von Schmuckarbeiten aus Edelmetall aus den Staatlichen Museen zu Berlin* (Berlin, 1932) 58, no. 15 a–b; 59, no. 16 a–b.
3. Hoffman and Davidson, *Greek Gold* 96, 98.

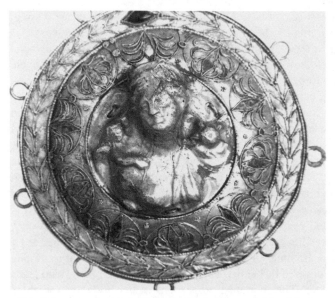

100. Hair ornament with Aphrodite and Eros, Museum of Art, Rhode
Island School of Design, Providence

101. Silver pin with Aphrodite and
Eros, Museum für Kunst und
Gewerbe, Hamburg

102. Earrings from Kyme, Antikenmuseum, West Berlin

103. Earrings from Kalymnos, Antikenmuseum, West Berlin

143

104. Circe's house from the Odyssey Frieze, Vatican Museum

Magic certainly played a part in the Hellenistic aesthetic. Unfortunately, we do not have in surviving texts and works of art so much evidence of this as we should like. The miniature hunchbacks and dwarfs with their exaggerated phalloi were almost certainly good-luck or apotropaic pieces.[4] In the Odyssey Frieze a magic wheel hangs from the lintel of Circe's doorway, and the branches that are stuck in the ground before her house are also thought to be of magical significance (fig. 104).[5]

In literature, as presaged by the fourth-century earrings described above, magic is associated with romantic love. Jason in *Argonautica* III wins the fleece by the witchcraft that Medea out of her passion had taught him. When she brought him the charm (φάρμακον 1014) from out of her girdle,[6] the poet adds that she would have drawn all her soul from out of her breast and given it to him in her delight at his desire (1015–16). In Book IV Circe's purification of Jason and Medea smacks more of archaic religious ritual than it does of magic, but she is herself clearly a sorceress, which is akin to being

4. See Chapter 5, note 1.
5. Von Blanckenhagen, "The Odyssey Frieze," 107.
6. R. J. Clark, "A Note on Medea's Plant and the Mandrake," *Folklore* 79 (1968) 227–31, argues that this φάρμακον is the mandrake, supposed to be an aphrodisiac because its root has shoots resembling human genitalia.

a seductress of men. When Jason and Medea came upon her, she was bathing her head in the salty sea-spray, for she had been frightened by her dreams in the night. Her rooms and the walls of the palace had been running with blood, and flames were destroying all the drugs (φάρμακ') with which she bewitched (θέλγ') whatever strangers came (662–77). And she is followed by the creatures she has transformed. They are not like wild beasts, nor yet like men, but are composed of a medley of limbs. This is magic of a dire sort.

Less horrible by far is the magic worked in Theocritus' *Idyll* II. Simaetha, who was too easily won and has been abandoned by her heartless lover, practices a witchcraft that seems at once designed to do him harm and to win him back. The rites she performs have their parallels in the magic papyri; we can therefore be sure that Theocritus is incorporating into his very artful poem the actual practices of real people: binding a bowl with fillets of wool, burning barley groats and bay and bran, melting wax, whirling the rhombus, burning the fringe from Delphis' cloak, braying a lizard, kneading herbs on Delphis' threshold.[7] The first refrain—"Magic wheel, draw to my house that man of mine"—tells us that throughout the first half of the poem Simaetha is working the iynx, the very instrument that we saw in the hands of the Erotes on the golden earrings. It was, as Pindar tells us (*Pyth.* IV.214), the invention of Aphrodite. Its magic then was specifically for the purposes of love.[8] The eroticism of *Idyll* II is created in part by the iynx refrain,[9] which by its very repetition suggests a climax; in part by the description of Delphis and Eudamippus walking together, their beards more golden than helichryse and their breasts more shining than the moon (78–79); and most of all of course by the seduction scene itself, which is more suggestive than explicit: "And quickly flesh warmed to flesh, our faces were hotter than before, and we were whispering sweetly, and—not to babble on too long, dear Moon—ἐπράχθη τὰ μέγιστα, καὶ ἐς πόθον ἤνθομες ἄμφω (*literally,* the greatest things were accomplished and we two came to our desire)" (140–43).

The brevity of the seduction scene itself contrasts with that of *Idyll* XXVII, which is certainly not by Theocritus and may even fall within the early Christian era.[10] Daphnis has stolen a kiss from a girl who wipes her mouth and spits it out. He reminds her that she will not always be young. She admits that she grows older but for the time she drinks milk and honey. Your grape, he

7. Gow, *Theocritus* II, 41–48.
8. Cf. C. Segal, "Simaetha and the Iynx (Theocritus, *Idyll* II)," reprinted from *Quaderni Urbinati di Cultura Classica* 15 (1973) 32–43 in *Poetry and Myth in Ancient Pastoral* 73–84, who sees the iynx as symbolic of seduction rather than marriage.
9. G. Lawall, "Simaetha's Incantation: Structure and Imagery," *Transactions of the American Philological Association* 92 (1961) 283–94, shows that *Idyll* II has a structure of three climaxes developed from incantation but does not suggest that the climaxes themselves may be seen as erotic.
10. Gow, *Theocritus* II, 485.

tells her, will become a raisin and what is now a rose will wither and die. She gives a number of excuses. Marriages are full of troubles. Wives are afraid of their husbands. She fears the pains of childbirth. She is afraid of losing her looks. Finally he persuades her to come see how his slender cypresses grow. She looses her goats and goes. The scene that follows is delightfully erotic:

> *Girl:* What are you doing, satyr-boy? Why do you touch my breasts inside my dress?
> *Daphnis:* I'll give those velvety apples of yours their first lesson.
> *Girl:* I'm fainting, by Pan. Take your hand out again.
> *Daphnis:* Courage, dear girl. Why do you tremble? How timid you are!
> *Girl:* You throw me in the ditch and dirty my pretty dress.
> *Daphnis:* I put a soft fleece here beneath your clothes.
> *Girl:* Oh dear, you've torn my sash too. Why did you undo it?
>
> . . . .
>
> *Girl:* You've made my cloak a rag. I'm naked.
>
> (49–59)

There is wit here, and that as well as the gradual undressing of the girl is a part of the eroticism. The quality of her flesh is deliciously suggested by describing her breasts as velvety (χνοάοντα 50) apples. The verb is elsewhere used of the down when it first appears on a young man's cheeks and of the bloom on fruit. The representation of female flesh is a major achievement of the Hellenistic sculptors. In this poem the same is accomplished, here by the "velvety apples," and earlier, obliquely, by the mention of grapes, roses, milk, and honey—all that is sweet and luscious.

Dioscorides, who died probably at the end of the third century B.C., has left us epigrams of an amatory nature which are notable for their evocation of both male and female flesh. In X (*AP* 12.37) he tells us that Eros, murderer of men, teasingly (παίζων) molded (soft as) marrow (μυελίνην) the buttocks of Sosarchus of Amphipolis, wanting to provoke Zeus, because his thighs are much more honeyed (μελιχρότεροι) than those of Ganymede. Epigram I (*AP* 5.56) is even more remarkable for its sensuous language, particularly its compounds. "They drive one wild," the poet says, "those rosy (ῥοδόχροα) lips, prattling soul-melting (ψυχοτακῆ) portals of an ambrosial mouth, the eyes that flash beneath heavy brows . . . the milky (γλαγόεντες) breasts, well-mated, desirable (ἱμερόεντες), finely formed, more delightful than any bud (κάλυκος)." Still more erotic are the first two lines of epigram V (*AP* 5.55): "Stretching Doris with her rosy buttocks (ῥοδόπυγον) across my bed, I become immortal in her dewy blossoms (ἄνθεσιν ἐν χλοεροῖς)." [11] Here again is the evocation of female flesh. The rest of the poem, which is a fairly

---

11. G. Zanker, *Realism in Alexandrian Poetry* (London, Sydney, and Wolfeboro, N.H., 1987) 163, finds this poem "purely comic."

105. Aphrodite or nymph, Rhodes Museum

explicit description of their love-making, is, because it is less suggestive, less erotic.

The most sensuous representations in sculpture of female flesh date to the second century B.C. The seated torso (ca. 150 B.C.) of a nymph, or possibly Aphrodite, from Rhodes is one of the finest examples (fig. 105). The twist of the torso, the deliciously rounded belly rising above the draperies that cover her thighs, knees, and lower legs, the upward thrust of her little breasts set off

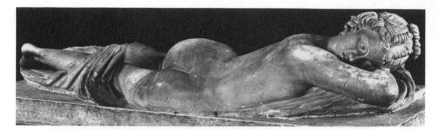

106. Sleeping Hermaphrodite, Museo Nazionale delle Terme, Rome

by the draperies that cover her back and left shoulder are a version in marble of Dioscorides' sensuous epigrams.

Certainly one of the most erotic of sculptures is that of the Sleeping Hermaphrodite in the Museo Nazionale, Rome, the original of which dated to 200–150 B.C. (fig. 106). Surely there is nowhere in Hellenistic art a more sensuous pair of buttocks than these. They rival those of Dioscorides' rosy-bottomed (ῥοδόπυγον) Doris.

The representation of sleep was another of the Hellenistic sculptors' major achievements. This is often but another aspect of the erotic. The sleeping satyr in the Glyptothek, Munich, is one example (fig. 107). Another is the head of a sleeping woman in the Museo Nazionale delle Terme at Rome (fig. 108). It is perhaps the vulnerability of these sleeping figures that makes them so especially sensuous. The Sleeping Eros in the Metropolitan Museum, New York, which also dates to about 200 B.C., is both realistically childlike and in his sensuous abandon suggestive of all that he provokes (fig. 109). The torsion of his plump little body, the spread of his equally plump thighs and of his exquisitely rendered toes all represent the sexuality as well as the innocence of childhood. Even the full, sensuous features of his face belie the sweet innocence of his expression.

Sleep and Eros were a favorite theme of Meleager. "If anyone lies beneath Heliodora's cloak," he says to his fellow reveller, Lady Night, "warmed by her flesh that cheats sleep, let the lamp sleep and let him, asleep on her breast, lie a second Endymion" (LI; *AP* 5.165). Again, he addresses Zenophila: "You're sleeping, Zenophila, my tender bloom. I wish that I were a wingless sleep to come beneath your eyelids so that not even he who lulls the eyes of Zeus could come to you, but only I alone" (XXXVI; *AP* 5.174). And twice he prevails upon mosquitoes, once to let Zenophila sleep a little in peace. But why does he beg in vain? "Even pitiless wild beasts enjoy the warmth of her tender flesh" (XXXIII; *AP* 5.151). On another occasion he sends the mosquito as a courier. "May you light on the tip of Zenophila's ear and whisper this: 'Sleepless he waits for you. But you, you lazy girl, forget your loves and sleep' " (XXXIV; *AP* 5.152).

Eros as a child, even as an infant, is a popular theme among the Hellenistic

107. Sleeping satyr, Staatliche Antikensammlungen und Glyptothek, Munich

epigrammatists. Asclepiades (XV; *AP* 12.46) asks the Erotes why they burn him, for if he dies (τι πάθω), what will they do? Clearly, the silly things will play at knucklebones just as they did before. Meleager (XV; *AP* 12.47) says that Eros, the baby still in his mother's lap, playing at dice in the morning, played away his soul. It is Meleager (LVIII; *AP* 5.187) too who gives us the most realistic picture of a baby; in this case the infant happens to be Eros: "Sell it," he says, "even though it sleeps still on its mother's breast. Sell it! . . . . It has a pug nose and little wings and with its nails it scratches sharply. In the midst of its crying it bursts out laughing. Besides, no one can suckle it. It's forever prattling, looking about, a savage creature. Its own mother can't tame it. A monster in every way!"

108. Sleeping Woman, Museo
Nazionale delle Terme, Rome

109. Sleeping Eros, Metropolitan Museum of Art, New York

The mighty power of the tiny creature Eros is a favorite theme in Hellenistic literature and art.[12] The *Anthology* has many poems like those above, and they were anticipated—or perhaps succeeded[13]—by a Pseudo-Theocritean *Idyll* (XIX), in which Eros was stung by a bee while he was stealing honey

12. Onians 128.
13. See Gow, *Theocritus* II, 362.

110. Young centaur, Palazzo dei Conservatori, Rome

from the hives. "He blew on his hand, and stamped the ground, and danced
up and down. He showed his hurt to Aphrodite and complained that so small a
creature as a bee could cause such a wound. And his mother laughed. 'Aren't
you just like the bees, who are so small and deal such wounds?'" (3–8).
We see the same motif in the painting and sculpture of the period. We have
Roman copies of Hellenistic originals of perhaps the second century B.C. of
two centaurs with small Erotes riding on their backs. One is jaunty and young
(fig. 110), but the other is old (fig. 111), has his hands tied behind his back,

111. Old centaur, Louvre, Paris

and displays on his anguished face the torment of love. He is entirely at the
mercy of the tiny Cupid on his back. So too the wall painting of Heracles and
Omphale from the house of Siricus at Pompeii, which may also derive from
a Hellenistic original, shows Erotes of an exaggeratedly small size. The scale
suggests the power of the tiny creatures over even the mighty Heracles.[14]

Onians, correctly I think, associates the popular theme of the thorn in
the foot with the wounding power of the little Eros.[15] In Theocritus' *Idyll* IV,
Battus, who has been discussing love affairs with his companion Corydon,
gets a thorn in his foot. Corydon removes it, and Battus says, "How little
the wound that masters so big a man!" (55). His foot stands surely for his
soul. Several sculptured groups of Pan removing a thorn from a satyr's foot

14. Onians 126 and fig. 124.
15. Ibid. 128.

112. Pan removing thorn from foot of satyr, Louvre, Paris

probably also make an oblique statement of the wounding power of love. In the groups from the Louvre (fig. 112) and the Vatican (fig. 113) the agonized faces of the satyrs suggest that the little thorn is Eros himself. These groups date probably to the first century B.C.

Toward the end of the Hellenistic period we have in the poet Meleager and in the sculpture of the period eroticism of a more sentimental nature. Meleager's verse is charming, often precious; too much of it becomes a diet of candied violets. It has its sensuous touches, however. Look, he says in XLII (*AP* 5.136), how the rose that is a lover of love (φιλέραστον) is weeping, because it sees Heliodora elsewhere and not in his bosom. In L (*AP* 5.163) he addresses a flower-feasted bee and asks why it deserts the buds of spring and lights on Heliodora's skin. The sensuous sweetness of these epigrams is anticipated in the sculptured group of Eros and Psyche (The Capitoline Kiss)

113. Pan removing thorn from foot of satyr, Vatican Museum

in the Museo Capitolino, Rome, the original of which dated to the first half of the second century B.C. (fig. 114). Its very size (4′1″ or 1.25 m) makes it sentimentally appealing. As Charbonneaux points out, Eros' body recalls that of the sleeping Hermaphrodite and Psyche's the late-fourth-century type of the half-naked Aphrodite.[16] These facts alone make them erotic in their intention. The sensuous quality of their bodies is enhanced by their turning toward and embracing one another. The babyish smile on Eros' face, the tender tendrils of the hair of each, and the rather precious stance of Eros' feet and legs are much in the manner of Meleager's elegant but slightly sentimental verse.

16. Charbonneaux 316.

114. Eros and Psyche, Palazzo dei Conservatori, Rome

XI

Archaizing

Archaizing is one of the more appealing mannerisms of Hellenistic relief sculpture.[1] Bodies conceived in three dimensions are clothed in draperies that are diaphanous and yet pressed flat to form highly stylized zigzag patterns; they reveal but do not at all follow the curves of the figures beneath. The effect is decorative and gay, a delightful blending of the old and the new. The style is, as Havelock observes, associated with the dance. Its mood is pastoral, joyous rather than reverential.[2] Is there a corresponding technique in the poetry of the Hellenistic period? I think that there is, but it does not occur in the places or in the way that one at first supposes it may.

There is no doubt that the Hellenistic poets looked to the past in their selections of genres. Apollonius wrote epic; Callimachus hymns, which were to some degree modelled on the Homeric *Hymns*. Theocritus seems to have invented his form, the pastoral, but in bordering upon mock-epic in certain

---

1. On the dating of archaistic sculpture see E. Schmidt, *Archaistische Kunst in Griechenland und Rom* (Munich, 1922); G. Becatti, "Lo stile arcaistico," *La Critica d'Arte: Rivista Bimestrale di Arti Figurative per il Mondo Antico* 6 (1941) 32–48; W. Fuchs, *Die Vorbilder der neuattischen Reliefs: Jahrbuch des Deutschen Archäologischen Instituts*, Erganzungsheft 20 (1959); and especially C. M. Havelock, "Archaistic Reliefs of the Hellenistic Period," *American Journal of Archaeology* 68 (1964) 43–58, and "The Archaic as Survival versus the Archaistic as a New Style," ibid. 69 (1965) 331–40. Havelock, in contrast to Schmidt and Fuchs and in accord with Becatti, sees true archaizing as a strictly Hellenistic phenomenon. Pollitt, *AHA* 180–84, gives a summary of the scholarship on the problem.

2. Havelock, "The Archaic as Survival," 339. E. B. Harrison, *Archaic and Archaistic Sculpture: The Athenian Agora XI* (Princeton, 1965) 64, declares, however, that "the purpose of the archaism is not to revive an art for which some kind of esthetic nostalgia is felt but to emphasize the venerability and permanence of existing institutions."

of his *Idylls*, he by definition looks back to Homer, and this is evident in his choice of epic language. Aratus obviously modelled his didactic poem not only upon the prose works of Eudoxus and Theophrastus but also upon Hesiod's *Works and Days*. Even the elegists of the *Anthology* built upon a tradition founded in part by the archaic elegists, in part by the early lyricists.

Yet, the differences between these Hellenistic poets and their predecessors are more striking than the similarities. Apollonius writes an epic that is episodic rather than structured around a central theme such as the wrath of Achilles or the homecoming of Odysseus. The central theme may be the quest for the fleece, but the actual winning of the fleece occupies but a small part of Book III. The overall impression is that of a voyage. The poem in its descriptions of exotic peoples and places reminds us more of Herodotus than it does of Homer. Even the similes—which are often Homeric in subject matter, dealing with wolves, lions, oxen, bees, hounds, horses—are remarkable for the difference of their shape. They are not, like Homer's, "long-tailed." Even when Apollonius is describing an Homeric action, such as a ship's setting sail, he deliberately varies the language. Where Homer is swift and simple, Apollonius is specific and circumstantial.[3]

Callimachus' *Hymns* are at their best burlesque, and at their worst— to modern taste, at least—aetiological. The Callimachean *Hymns* also lack the limpidity, the speed, the simplicity, and, for the most part, the magical qualities of the archaic *Hymns*. They abound in proper names, learned allusions, and references which are to us obscure. Aratus writes a didactic poem which includes weather signs for farmers, but his work, while reminiscent of Hesiod's *Works and Days* in purpose and content, is quite different in style. His Greek is crabbed; Hesiod's is of epic clarity.

Archaizing does not then in the Hellenistic poets consist in the selection of genre or even in the borrowings of epic language. These elements are more correctly seen as simply traditional. All poets after Homer to one degree or another incorporated his language. Rather, archaizing is to be seen in Callimachus and more especially in Apollonius in passages which preserve the sense of the sweetness and the magic of nature, in what may be thought of as the decorative elements in their poetry. In Aratus the problem is more

---

3. There have been many studies of Homeric influence in Apollonius. Among recent essays dealing with the similes are J. F. Carspecker, "Apollonius Rhodius and the Homeric Epic," *Yale Classical Studies* 13 (1952) 58–99; A. W. James, "Some Examples of Imitation in the Similes of Later Greek Epic," *Antichthon* 3 (1969) 77–90; and R. W. Garson, "Homeric Echoes in Apollonius Rhodius' *Argonautica*," *Classical Philology* 67 (1972) 1–9. On Homeric influence in general upon Apollonius see also A. W. Bulloch, "Apollonius Rhodius, *Argonautica* 2, 177: A Case-Study in Hellenistic Poetic Style," *Hermes* 101 (1973) 496–98, and J. W. Shumacher, "Homeric Transformations in the *Argonautica* of Apollonius of Rhodes" (diss. Univ. of Pennsylvania, 1969).

complicated. There, it is as though the Hesiodic elements were the archaistic draperies cloaking a three-dimensional form which is Stoicism.[4]

In his *Hymn to Apollo* (II) Callimachus touches upon the magical healing and life-giving powers of a gold-bedecked Apollo in a manner that is reminiscent of the Homeric *Hymns*: "Golden is his tunic, his cloak, his lyre and his Lycian bow and his quiver; of gold are his sandals too. Apollo is rich in gold and rich in possessions as well. From Pytho you could tell" (32–35). Gold, especially in Pindar but in the lyric poets as well, is a standard attribute of gods, but the detailing here of Apollo's possessions recalls the gold-filleted Hours' bedecking of Aphrodite in the Homeric *Hymn* (VI) dedicated to her: "They clothed her in ambrosial garments, and on her head they put a lovely garland of gold. In the pierced lobes of her ears they put ornaments of orichalc and precious gold. They adorned her tender neck and shining white breasts with golden necklaces, with which the gold-filleted Hours adorn themselves when they go to the lovely dance of the gods and their father's house" (6–13).

Callimachus continues his description of the gold-bedecked Apollo. "He is forever beautiful and forever young. Never has there come to the girlish cheeks of Phoebus the slightest down. His locks distill fragrant oils on the ground. Not fat does the hair of Apollo distill but all-healing itself. In the city where those dews fall to the ground all things become free from harm" (36–41). This is a ritualistic description of Apollo; it tells us specifically what his healing powers are. It does, however, recall—though with diminished force —the magical effect that divinities have upon the phenomena of nature in the Homeric *Hymns*. When Artemis in XXVII shoots her arrows over the shadowy hills and windy peaks, "the tops of the high mountains tremble and the tangled wood echoes terribly with the cries of wild beasts and the earth trembles and the sea with its fishes" (6–9). In XXVIII nature responds still more remarkably to the birth of Athene. "Mighty Olympus began to reel awesomely at the might of the gray-eyed goddess, and all around the earth echoed terribly, and the sea, tossed with its bluc-black waves, shifted" (9–12).

In the Callimachean hymn Apollo as Nomios promotes fertility. "Easily would the pasturing cattle grow more, nor would the she-goats lack young if Apollo cast his eye upon them when they fed, nor would the ewes be without milk or barren, but all would have lambs at their feet, and the one who bore one would bear two" (50–54). The magic of his life-giving power here recalls

4. On Hesiodic and Stoic influence see W. Ludwig, "Die *Phainomena* Arats als hellenistische Dichtung," *Hermes* 91 (1963) 425–48; W. Sale, "The Popularity of Aratus," *Classical Journal* 61 (1965) 160–64; B. Effe, "Προτέρη γενεή: Ein stoische Hesiod-interpretation in Arats *Phainomena*," *Rheinisches Museum für Philologie* 113 (1970) 167–82; A. W. James, "The Zeus Hymns of Cleanthes and Aratus," *Antichthon* 6 (1972) 28–38; H. Schwabl, "Zur Mimesis bei Arat: Prooimion und Parthenos," in *Antidosis: Festschrift für W. Kraus*, ed. R. Hanslik, A. Lesky, and H. Schwabl (Vienna, 1972) 336–56; G. Luck, "Aratea," *American Journal of Philology* 97 (1976) 213–34.

that of Demeter, who in the Homeric *Hymn* II, when Zeus had granted her wishes, rushed down to the plain of Rharus, once fertile but now by the designs of the goddess idle and totally leafless. "But afterward, as spring came on, it was to wave with long ears of corn, and on the ground its rich furrows were to be loaded with grain, and others would be bound already in sheaves" (453–56). The brief descriptions of Apollo's magic in the Callimachean hymn may be seen as a form of archaizing.

Another archaizing touch is the description in Callimachus' *Hymn to Artemis* (III) of the Amazons dancing. "They themselves danced around the image, first among the shields in armor, and then arranging in a circle a wide chorus. The high-pitched pipes played a shrill accompaniment that they might beat (ῥήσσωσιν) the ground together. For not yet had they pierced the bones of the fawn, Athene's work, a bane to deer. The echo reached Sardis and the Berecynthian range. They with their feet beat loudly (οὖλα κατεκροτάλιζον), and their quivers rattled" (240–47). This is a particularly vivid picture of dancing, enhanced by the onomatopoeia in the second expression. Archaizing in sculpture is associated with the dance, and this passage may be an example of such in poetry, for the Homeric *Hymn to the Pythian Apollo* (III) also offers an enchanting picture of the dance. There, "the lovely-haired Graces and the merry Seasons and Harmonia and Hebe and Aphrodite, daughter of Zeus, dance, holding one another by the wrist (ὀρχεῦντ' ἀλλήλων ἐπὶ καρπῷ χεῖρας ἔχουσαι), and among them sings one not mean nor slight but tall to see and wondrous in her beauty, Artemis, who delights in arrows and is sister to Apollo. And among them sport (παίζουσ') Ares and the Keen-sighted Slayer of Argus, but Phoebus Apollo plays his lyre, stepping beautifully and high (καλὰ καὶ ὕψι βιβάς)" (194–202).

Callimachus in his *Hymn to Delos* (IV) adds to his list of places that shunned Leto in her travail the earth-born nymph Melia, who "whirled about and ceased from her dance, and her cheek grew pale as she panted for her age-mate oak when she saw the locks of Helicon shaken." "My goddesses," says the poet, "tell me, Muses, were the oaks born when the Nymphs were? The Nymphs rejoice when the rain causes the oaks to grow. In turn, the Nymphs weep when there are no longer leaves on the oaks" (79–85). This does look like a deliberate piece of archaizing. Not only were dancing Nymphs—or Graces or Seasons—a favorite subject of the archaistic sculptors, but this passage seems consciously to recall one in the Homeric *Hymn to Aphrodite* (V). There, the goddess promises that the child she has conceived will be reared by "the deep bosomed mountain Nymphs, who live for a long time, eat ambrosia, and tread the lovely dance (καλὸν χορὸν ἐρρώσαντο) with the gods. . . . Together with them at their birth the pines and the high-topped oaks spring up on the fertile earth, beautiful and flourishing upon the lofty mountains. They stand tall and men call them the precincts of the immortals, and mortals do not fell them with the axe. But when the lot of death stands near, first those lovely trees wither where they stand, their bark shrivels around them, their branches fall, and the souls of the Nymphs and the trees leave the light of the sun at the same time" (257–72). Here we have the dance and in the association of nymph and tree the magical aspect of nature that is a mark of the archaic hymns and which Callimachus in his hymn is almost certainly trying to reproduce or at least recall.

Apollonius, like Callimachus, when he evokes the sweetness of nature, is reminiscent of the lyric poets. He is also, like Callimachus, reminiscent of the Homeric *Hymns* and even of Pindar in his similes and other descriptions. In Book I he likens the Argonauts at their departure, smiting the sea with oars, to youths dancing. Just as they "set up a dance to Phoebus in either Pytho or Ortygia or by the waters of Ismenus and in time with the lyre they together around the altar beat the ground with their quick feet (φόρμιγγος ὑπαὶ περὶ βωμὸν ὁμαρτῇ / ἐμμελέως κραιπνοῖσι πέδον ῥήσσωσι πόδεσσιν), so they at the lyre of Orpheus beat with their oars the rushing water of the sea and the surge washed over the blades. On this side and on that the black (κελαινή) brine seethed with foam, roaring terribly at the strength of the mighty men. Their armor flashed like flame in the sun as the ship took its course, and far behind their wake was ever white (ἐλευκαίνοντο), like a path one sees over a green (χλοεροῖο) plain" (537–46).

Just as the image of the dance recalls both archaistic reliefs and the description of the Graces and their companions dancing in the Homeric *Hymn to Apollo*, so here the joy of the departure and the flashing light and color of the armor, the sun, and the sea remind one of the Homeric *Hymn to Dionysus* (VII), which is also remarkable for its use of words denoting or suggesting color. Dionysus' hair was blue-black (κυάνεαι 5); his robe was crimson (πορφύρεον 6); the sea was sparkling (οἶνοπα 7); Dionysus' eyes were dark (κυανέοισι 15); the land was black (μελαίνης 22). All this contributes to the magic and the charm of this early hymn. Apollonius, when he achieves a similar effect, is archaizing.[5]

He may also be archaizing when at the end of this description he tells of Chiron coming down from the mountain top to the sea, where he dipped his feet in the white surf of the breaking wave (πολιῇ δ' ἐπὶ κύματος ἀγῇ / τέγγε πόδας I.554–55), and waving often with his broad hand called out to wish them at their departure a happy homecoming. With him his wife, carrying Peleus' son Achilles on her arm, showed the child to his dear father. One remembers Pindar, who wrote often of Chiron as a mentor to young heroes, and especially *Nemean* III.46–49, where Achilles slew lions and wild boars and dragged their panting bodies back to the Centaur, for the first time when he was six years old—and then ever after. Babies occur in the archaic poets

5. See Fowler, "The Archaic Aesthetic."

and then not again in literature until the Hellenistic period. The infant Achilles here in the arms of Chiron's wife is another archaizing touch.[6] So too is the picture of Chiron wetting his toes in the surf. It has the naive charm of the tortoise in the Homeric *Hymn to Hermes* (IV), who is feeding on the rich grass in front of the house, waddling along (σαῦλα ποσὶν βαίνουσα 28).

Another archaizing touch in Apollonius is the account of the miracles that occurred at the Argonauts' worship of Rhea. "The trees shed fruit in unending abundance, and at their feet the earth of itself put forth flowers from the delicate grass. The wild beasts left their lairs and their thickets and came up, fawning with their tails" (I.1142–45). The magic of this does not match but is perhaps meant to recall that of the Homeric *Hymn to Dionysus* (VII), where "first of all," on the pirates' ship that carried the god, "fragrant wine, sweet to drink, burbled throughout the swift black ship and there arose an ambrosial odor. . . . And straightway at the very top of the mast there spread a vine, on this side and on that, and there hung down from it many clusters, and dark ivy wound around the mast, blossoming with flowers, and lovely fruit grew upon it, and all the tholepins were covered with garlands" (35–42).

Apollonius may have been inspired by the same or a similar work when he described the robe of Hypsipyle, which Jason and Medea planned to give to Apsyrtus. "You could never by touching or looking satisfy your sweet desire. An ambrosial odor arose from it, from the time when the Nysian himself lay upon it, flushed with wine and nectar, clasping the lovely breasts of the virgin daughter of Minos, whom Theseus had left behind on the island of Dia when she followed him from Knossos" (IV.429–34). This kind of sensuous magic is typical of the Homeric *Hymns*. When it appears in Apollonius, it is a form of archaizing.

These passages describing the magical sweetness of nature, the dance of the Amazons, the bedecking of divinities in golden garments and jewelry —all of them reminiscent of the Homeric *Hymns* and even of Pindar—are easily likened to the Dance of Dionysus and the Seasons that appears on a Roman copy of a Greek original, perhaps a painting rather than a sculptured relief, dating to about 200 B.C. (fig. 115). Here, the dancing figures are set in contrasting poses; Spring turns toward us; Summer pivots away; Autumn is again made to face in our direction. Their three-dimensional bodies are clothed in draperies which are transparent over their breasts, buttocks, and legs but which thicken unrealistically in zigzags and swallow tails as they leave the bodies and swing, decoratively rather than naturalistically, in the air. These artifically conceived swathes and trains together with the delicately arched feet of the dancers create a mood of gaiety. The flowers in Spring's apron, the sheaf of wheat in Summer's hand suggest too the wondrous fertility of nature. By

6. See Fowler, "The Centaur's Smile," 159–70.

115. Dance of Dionysus and the Seasons, Louvre, Paris

contrast, the votive relief in the Acropolis Museum, Athens, showing Hermes leading "the lovely-haired daughters of Zeus dancing lightly" depicts the three maidens in a typically archaic pose (fig. 116). Their upper bodies face the spectator, while their lower limbs are shown completely in profile. Their feet are absolutely flat, as are Hermes' and those of the child who follows—out of step. Their draperies are transparent from top to bottom, but the crinkles do not follow the lines of their rather muscular bodies. Neither do they swirl realistically. They hang for the most part straight down. Hermes' clothing, on the other hand, swathes his figure closely. We have here the naive charm of the true archaic. It is the difference between the Homeric *Hymns* or Hesiod and Apollonius.

Aratus' archaizing—that is, his imitation of Hesiod—is better compared to the marble tripod base of Heracles, Dionysus, and a Maenad in the Agora Museum, which dates to about 100 B.C. (figs. 117–19).[7] Heracles and Dionysus stand stiffly, their knees locked, their feet quite flat on the ground. Their buttocks as a result protrude at an exaggerated angle. The Maenad has the superciliously arched feet of the typically archaistic figure, and her garments swing in pleated zigzags both forward and backward in an impossible,

7. These were the original identifications. Harrison, *Archaic and Archaistic Sculpture*, 79–81, suggests, however, that the male figure with the club is Theseus and the other two figures perhaps Aigeus and Medea.

116. The Lovely-haired Daughters of Zeus Dancing Lightly, Acropolis Museum, Athens

though not totally unattractive, manner. These awkward yet appealing three-dimensional figures clothed in highly stylized, two-dimensional draperies are not unlike Aratus' Stoicism clothed in Hesiodic garb.

Hesiod's poem, though it belongs to the epic tradition, is certainly archaic rather than heroic in its outlook. The sense of inherited guilt anticipates that of Solon, and the emphasis on cleansings, ritual, and superstitions is a part of what Dodds meant by "messy archaic rituals" that he saw as typical of a "guilt culture." [8] There is more question about Aratus' Stoicism. Wilamowitz, for instance, has reservations about the Stoicism of his prologue.[9] If, however, the prologue is considered in conjunction with the rest of the poem, it is obvious that in declaring the streets, the marketplaces, the harbors, and the sea full (μεσταὶ . . . μεστή 2–3) of Zeus, Aratus is pronouncing Stoic doctrine, for Stoicism is, I believe, implicit in all the content and especially in the arrangement of the *Phaenomena*.

Aratus begins his poem with a prologue to Zeus, the god who is Logos,

8. E. R. Dodds, *The Greeks and the Irrational* (Berkeley and Los Angeles, 1951) 36.
9. U. von Wilamowitz, *Hellenistische Dichtung* II (Berlin, 1924) 262–66.

117. Heracles, tripod base, Agora
Museum, Athens

118. Dionysus, tripod base, Agora
Museum, Athens

164

119. Maenad, tripod base, Agora
Museum, Athens

which is the divine fire. He moves on to the heavenly bodies: the constellations, the planets, the circles of the celestial sphere, the risings and settings
of the stars, and the signs of the zodiac. All these are composed of the divine
fire and are in their orderly movements a perfect example of the "causal nexus
which controls cosmic events." [10] Aratus then goes on to the weather signs. He
begins by showing how the heavenly bodies warn sailors of a coming storm.
Man is the next object in the Great Chain of Being. In him nature (physis)
takes the form of reason (logos). From there Aratus moves to a description
of the behavior of creatures that heralds rain. These, the birds, the animals,
the insects, are next in the Stoic hierarchy. The divine fire in them takes the
form of "soul" as opposed to "reason." Plants, which have only "nature"
(physis), are mentioned but briefly (1044–63) and not last, which would be
their natural place in a Stoic design.[11] The disorder of the end of the poem
may be, as Couat suggests, an imitation of the disordered end of Hesiod's
Works and Days, in other words, a piece of deliberate archaizing.[12] In general,
however, the poem does preserve the Stoic conception of the universe: God,

10. A. A. Long, *Hellenistic Philosophy* (London, 1974) 130.
11. Ibid. 148.
12. A Couat, *Alexandrian Poetry under the First Three Ptolemies, 324–222 B.C.*, trans.
J. Loeb (London, 1931) 485.

Stars, Man, Creatures, all of them sharing in diminishing power the Divine Fire which is Logos.

The *Phaenomena* may be seen as Stoic in another sense too. Stoic philosophy was "rooted in the observation of particular phaenomena." It maintained "that all existing things are particulars." [13] Nothing could be more particular than the Weather Signs. It may well be the Stoic notion that animals have souls, irrational though they may be, that accounts for the anthropomorphizing treatment of the creatures in Aratus' poem and in the Hellenistic mosaicists as well. Those octopi look at us out of human eyes.

Aratus begins his poem: "From Zeus let us begin. Him never let us men leave unnamed. Full of Zeus are all the paths, all the markets of men, full the sea and the harbors"(1–4). Both the word ἄρρητον "unnamed" and the repetition in μεσταί . . . μεστή "full" are reminiscent of the prologue to the *Works and Days*. Hesiod invokes the Muses but then asks them to tell of Zeus and chant his praise. Through him men are famed and unfamed (ἄφατοί τε φατοί τε 3), named and unnamed (ῥητοί τ' ἄρρητοι 4). Easily (ῥέα 5) he makes a man strong, easily (ῥέα 5) he crushes the strong man, easily (ῥεῖα) he humbles the conspicuous and raises the obscure, easily (ῥεῖα 6) he straightens the crooked and withers the proud—Zeus who thunders on high. Aratus imitates the repetitions and borrows vocabulary (ἄρρητον 2). Hesiod's prologue enters immediately upon the archaic view of the world. Life is hard; prosperity is precarious; guilty men abound but receive their just deserts sooner or later. "Hear, see, and listen," he tells Perses, "and give straight judgments with justice" (9). This presages the moral tone of his poem. Aratus, on the other hand, proceeds from his opening to say that Zeus has given signs to men to tell them when the soil is best for the ox and the mattock, and when the seasons are favorable for planting trees and casting all manner of seeds. This tells us that he intends to write a poem like Hesiod's and can be taken as a piece of archaizing. Next he makes a statement that sounds Stoic: "For he himself set the signs in heaven, marking the constellations, and determined for the year what stars should most of all mark for men signs of the seasons that all things might grow unfailingly" (10–13). This is Zeus setting up his causal nexus: god, stars, man, animals, plants. Aratus' prologue, then, is a Stoic preamble decked out in Hesiodic trappings. It is his form of archaizing.

Since in the Weather Signs Aratus is following Theophrastus, there are no verbal echoes of the *Works and Days*. Aratus never rises to the lyricism of Hesiod describing the cuckoo when it first calls in the leaves of the oak and gives joy to man over the boundless earth (ἦμος κόκκυξ κοκκύζει δρυὸς ἐν πετάλοισι / τὸ πρῶτον, τέρπει δὲ βροτοὺς ἐπ' ἀπείρονα γαῖαν 486–87), or the winter winds that roar so that "beasts shudder and put their tails between their legs, even those whose hides are bound with fur" (511–14), or

13. Long, *Hellenistic Philosophy* 119, 141.

again spring, "when the artichoke blooms and the shrilling cicada sits in the tree and sheds his high-pitched song from under his wings in the season of wearying heat when goats are fattest and the wine best, women most wanton but men feeblest, since Sirius parches head and knees, and the skin is dry from the heat" (582–88). Still, the spirit and the intent of Aratus' signs are similar to Hesiod's. "Note," says Hesiod, "when you hear the voice of the crane crying year by year from the clouds above, for she gives the sign to plough and shows the season of rainy winter":

> φράζεσθαι δ', εὖτ' ἂν γεράνου φωνὴν ἐπακούσῃς
> ὑψόθεν ἐκ νεφέων ἐνιαύσια κεκληγυίης·
> ἥτ' ἀρότοιό τε σῆμα φέρει καὶ χείματος ὥρην
> δεικνύει ὀμβρηροῦ.

(448–50)

The sweet simplicity of this is lost in Aratus' awkward Greek:

> χαίρει καὶ γεράνων ἀγέλαις ὡραῖος ἀροτρεὺς
> ὥριον ἐρχομέναις, ὁ δ ἄώριος αὐτίκα μᾶλλον·
> αὔτως γὰρ χειμῶνες ἐπέρχονται γεράνοισιν,
> πρώϊα μὲν καὶ μᾶλλον ὁμιλαδὸν ἐρχομένῃσιν
> πρώϊοι·αὐτὰρ ὅτ' ὀψὲ καὶ οὐκ ἀγεληδὰ φανεῖσαι
> πλειότερον φορέονται ἐπὶ χρόνον, οὐδ' ἅμα πολλαί,
> ἀμβολίῃ χειμῶνος ὀφέλλεται ὕστερα ἔργα.

(1075–81)

Mair translates this crabbed passage as follows: "In seasonable flight of thronging cranes rejoices the seasonable farmer: in untimely flight the untimely ploughman. For ever so winters follow the cranes: early winters, when their flight is early and in flocks: when they fly late and not in flocks, but over a long period in small bands, the later farming benefits by the delay of winter." [14] The passage is based on Theophrastus 38, but it is hard not to believe that Aratus had Hesiod also in mind. If so, his archaizing here is indeed like that on the tripod base (figs. 117–19), of which Mitchell says, "First, in order to imitate the clear patterned character of archaic relief, the sculptor purposely swelled the muscular outline and as a result the shape within would be emphasized. Secondly, since the linear and the naturalistic are opposed to each other at the outset, the battlefield would have to be precisely at their point of meeting— along the contours." [15] One sees in Aratus' lines the swelling and the exaggeration, the battle between Hesiod's linearity and his own naturalism. The result may be awkward, but it is not altogether unattractive.

14. A. W. Mair, *Aratus*, Loeb Classical Library (London and Cambridge, Mass., 1921; repr. 1960) 293.

15. C. Mitchell, "Stylistic Problems in Greek and Roman Archaistic Reliefs," *Harvard Studies in Classical Philology* 61 (1953) 75–76.

XII

Skenographia, Skiagraphia, and Phantasia

Χάρις, best translated as "charm," is assuredly a mark of Hellenistic poetry and art. Dionysius of Halicarnassus (*Isoc.* III) uses the word as a critical term for both literature and sculpture, for he compares the rhetorical art of Lysias to that of the sculptors Calamis and Callimachus on account of their delicacy and charm (τῆς λεπτότητος ἕνεκα καὶ τῆς χάριτος). Other writers of the Hellenistic period seem also to have applied critical terms to more than one art and so by implication to have recognized in them a common aesthetic. Among the most interesting of these terms are τόνος and ἁρμογή. In a startling passage the elder Pliny (*NH* XXXV.29) tells us that "quod inter haec (lumen) et umbras esset, appellarunt tonon, commissuras vero colorum et transitus harmogen" ("that which exists between light and shade they called *tonos,* while the juxtapositions of colors and the transitions [from one to another of them] they called *harmoge*") This use of the word *tonos* may have derived from what Quintilian (*Inst.* XII.10.4) called the "luminum umbrarumque rationem," the theory of light and shade formulated by Apollodorus in the fifth century B.C. and developed, presumably, by Zeuxis.[1] The term was probably taken from musical theory, where it meant the "pitch," resulting from the "stretching" of strings, at which a scale was played; it meant something like our term "key."[2] It is most likely, therefore, to have originated with the Pythagoreans. In the Hellenistic period, significantly, it became a Stoic term and referred to the

1. J. J. Pollitt, *The Ancient View of Greek Art* (New Haven and London, 1974) 271.
2. Ibid.

"tension in matter, which, during each universal cycle, created the natural and human forms of the world." [3] It is perhaps no accident that painting and music share this word with Stoic cosmology. It is one of our oblique indications of the pervasive but not always obvious influence of Stoicism in the Hellenistic arts.[4] Ἁρμογή, a joining or fitting together, which Pliny tells us meant the juxtaposition of colors and transitions from one of them to another, is also a term of literary criticism. Dionysius of Halicarnassus (*Comp.* VIII.22.23) used it to refer to the joining of clauses, words, and letters.

The play of light and shade, which seems to be what Pliny meant by *tonos* and *harmoge,* is almost certainly a description of what we would call chiaroscuro. The ancient term for this technique of shading, of giving, impressionistically, by the laying on of paints the illusion of a play of light upon surfaces of varying quality and depth, was *skiagraphia.*[5] A more straightforward method of suggesting depth in a painted surface was drawing or painting in perspective, and this technique the ancients called *skenographia.*[6] The Hellenistic painters used both, with ever-increasing success, in their representations of space.[7]

The Hediste stele is an early and original example of a Hellenistic Greek painting that attempts to create a third dimension by the use of both lighting and drawing in perspective (fig. 68). It dates to approximately the middle of the third century B.C. It is very poorly preserved, but we can see a door opening to a room beyond, which has at its end another open door. The attendant women and Hediste are both drawn at angles to suggest depth, but they are shown in conflicting, if effective, perspectives. Light coming from a single source at the left falls on the young woman's face and breasts, and on parts of her pillow and coverlet. Although this is not yet true chiaroscuro, there is a marked contrast of light and shade.

An earlier attempt to create by shading, that is, hatching, perspective is the Kazanlak mural in the tomb of a Thracian prince in Bulgaria. This, Bruno proposes, is the kind of *skiagraphia* employed by Apollodorus.[8]

3. Ibid.
4. Pollitt (ibid.) reminds us that many terms used of the visual arts derive from musical terminology: these include ῥυθμός, ἁρμονία, and even χρόα "color," "which in developed musical theory referred to tonal variations within a given scale (Aristoxenus, *Harm.* 24)."
5. Ibid. 251ff. For another view of *skiagraphia* see E. Keuls, "Skiagraphia Once Again," *American Journal of Archaeology* 79 (1975) 1–16, who defines it as a form of impressionism, and for a reply to her view, E. Pemberton, "A Note on Skiagraphia," ibid. 80 (1976) 82–84.
6. Pollitt, *The Ancient View* 240ff.
7. J. D. White, *Perspective in Ancient Drawing and Painting,* Society for the Promotion of Hellenic Studies, Supp. Paper no. 7 (London, 1956) 61–66, argues that in the Second Pompeian Style there is actually a single vanishing point. He discusses in particular paintings from the Casa del Labirintho, the Villa dei Ministeri, and the Villa of Publius Fannius Sinistor at Boscoreale. Onians 160 states, however, "There remains a doubt as to whether a full linear perspective system was in use in antiquity."
8. V. J. Bruno, *Form and Color in Greek Painting* (New York, 1977) 29.

The Roman copy of an earlier painting, dating to about 300 B.C., of Achilles surrendering Briseis gives us—because of its greater sophistication, scale, and state of preservation—a better idea of these same techniques (fig. 1). Here, there is an attempt to create perspective in the open door, slanting to the left, and its frame, slanting to the right; in the two rows of soldiers standing behind Achilles and Briseis, who are themselves placed behind Patroclus; in the soldiers' shields, one behind the other. Most remarkable, however, is the figure of Achilles, facing almost forward and very successfully foreshortened. The light in this painting comes realistically and consistently from the upper right and highlights the bronze bodies of Achilles and Patroclus and the yellow draperies of Briseis. Contrasting pastel shades of pink, blue, mauve, and yellow-green in the helmets, plumes, shields, and clothing of the soldiers in the rear draw one's eye back and at the same time enhance the richness of the reddish-brown bodies in the foreground and so add to our sense of depth in the painting. There is still here a certain naivete in technique, and that is a part of what gives this picture its extraordinary appeal.

Skenographia and *skiagraphia* were not literary terms. Yet one can see in the Hellenistic poets, especially in Apollonius of Rhodes, attempts to create these painterly effects.[9] They appear particularly in descriptions of what one commonly calls "nature," but also in those of buildings and cities.

In *Argonautica* III the heroes' approach to the city of Aietes owes much to Homer's account of Odysseus' arrival at the palace of the Phaeacians. There are some verbal parallels but more often a similarity of action and word order with deliberately varied vocabulary. A goddess covers Odysseus and the Argonauts with a mist to cloak their arrivals and removes it when the proper moment comes. Both Odysseus and the Argonauts stand amazed at what they behold—man-made structures and the magic of nature. Alcinous' palace is more out of fairy-land than is Aietes'. Almost the first thing said of it is that it had a gleam as of the sun or the moon (VII.84). It had a brazen threshold, and brazen walls were raised ἔνθα καὶ ἔνθα, / ἐς μυχὸν ἐξ οὐδοῦ (86–87). The expression is vague: here and there, from threshold to corner. It apparently means "everywhere—as far as the eye could see," or as Fitzgerald translates it, "bronze-paneled walls, at several distances, making a vista." [10] There was a molding (θριγκός) of dark blue (κυάνοιο) running round (περί). What the substance of the dark-blue molding was we are left to wonder. The doors were gold and so were their handles. The posts and lintels were of silver. Of gold and silver were the hounds, works of Hephaestus, that guarded the doorways.

Aietes' palace is far more modestly—and realistically—described. The heroes stand at the entrance and marvel at the wide gates and columns which

9. On Apollonius as a painterly poet see E. Phinney, Jr., "Hellenistic Painting and the Poetic Style of Apollonius," *Classical Journal* 62 (1966–67) 145–49; M. A. Elvira, "Apolonio de Rodas y la pintura del primer helenismo," *Archivo Español de Arqueología* 50–51 (1977–78) 33–46.

10. *Odyssey*, trans. R. Fitzgerald (New York, 1963) 113.

rise in order around the walls; high up on the palace a coping of stone rests on brazen column capitals:

εὐρείας τε πύλας καὶ κίονας οἳ περὶ τοίχους
ἑξείης ἄνεχον, θριγκὸς δ᾽ ἐφύπερθε δόμοιο
λαΐνεος χαλκέῃσιν ἐπὶ γλυφίδεσσιν ἀρήρει.
(*Argon*. III.216–18)

The language here is specific and reflects the Hellenistic interest in architecture. The gates are broad (εὐρείας); the columns are set in order (ἑξείης); the coping (θριγκός) is set on brazen column capitals (γλυφίδεσσιν). We have a more definite sense here than in Homer of height and depth. There, the height and the depth were perhaps greater but were the result of illusion and magic rather than of architectural technique.

Later in the same passage Apollonius tells us that here there is an inner court (μέσσαυλος), and around it, here and there (ἔνθα καὶ ἔνθα, the Homeric phrase) are many well-fitted (εὐπηγεῖς, also an Homeric word) doors and chambers, and all along (παρέξ) on either side (ἑκάτερθε) is a richly wrought (δαιδαλέη . . . τέτυκτο) gallery (235 37). On both sides lofty buildings stand obliquely:

λέχρις δ᾽αἰπύτεροι δόμοι ἔστασαν ἀμφοτέρωθεν.
(238)

Here again is an attempt to give not only details of the architectural construction, the height and width of the building, but in that adverb λέχρις (not a Homeric word) perspective—that is, *skenographia*.

Callimachus in *Aitia* II.43 (*De Siciliae urbibus*) shows a technical interest in building and surveying. A certain bird of prey, when the heron does not follow it, "bewitches a rising tower and the measuring cords when the surveyors cast it straight out to cut narrow alleys and level roads":

καὶ γὰρ ὁ βασκα[ί]νει πύργον ἐ[γειρόμεν]ον
γεωδαῖται καὶ σπάρτα διην[εκὲς εὖτε] βάλωνται,
στείνεα καὶ λευρὰς ὄφρα τάμ[ωσιν ὁ]δούς.
(II, fr. 43.63–64)

One can suppose that Callimachus here was attempting to give depth as well as height and breadth to his description. He is describing Vitruvius' *ichnographia* or "ground plan" and *orthographia* "plan in elevation";[11] he is suggesting in

---

11. Vitruvius I.1.1: "Species dispositionis, quae graece dicuntur ἰδέαι, sunt hae: ichnographia, orthographia, scaenographia. . . . Item scaenographia est frontis et laterum abscedentium adumbratio ad circinique centrum omnium linearum responsus." Pollitt (*The Ancient View* 230–31) translates: "The subcategories, which the Greeks call ἰδέαι, of composition are these: *ichnographia* [ground plan] *orthographia* [plan in elevation], and *scaenographia*. . . . And finally *scaenographia* is the semblance of a front and of sides receding into the background and the correspondence of all the lines [in this representation] to [a vanishing point at] the center of a circle."

120. Dionysus visiting a tragic poet, British Museum, London

the next two lines his *skenographia*. In another fragment Callimachus says:

καὶ γλαρίδες σταφύλη τε καθιεμένη τε μολυβδίς.

(512)

Trypanis translates this as "and the chisels and the plummet of a level and the sinking plumb of a mason's line." [12]

The Hellenistic period appears to have been the first to use professional architects who designed buildings in advance of construction, and we may have archaeological evidence of a ground plan: an inscription from Priene tells us that in the second century B.C. a certain Hermogenes dedicated at the temple of Athene "a hypographe of the temple, which he also executed." The hypographe may well have been the "ground plan." [13]

Relief sculpture in particular had grappled from the beginning with perspective, and in the relief in the British Museum from the early first century B.C. of Dionysus visiting a tragic poet we actually see buildings "aslant" (fig. 120). The Hellenistic painters also struggled to achieve perspective. This shows most clearly in the Roman architectural paintings from Boscoreale, which also date to the first century B.C. (fig. 121),[14] but we see it to some degree in both landscapes and buildings in all the Hellenistic wall paintings. The technique had improved remarkably since the days of the vase-painters,

12. C. A. Trypanis, *Callimachus*, Loeb Classical Library (Cambridge, Mass., and London, 1958) 259.

13. J. J. Coulton, *Ancient Greek Architects at Work* (Ithaca, N.Y., 1977) 17, 29, 66–73.

14. See note 7.

121. Wall painting from the House of Publius Fannius Synistor, Boscoreale, Metropolitan Museum of Art, New York

and this pride in technique is reflected as early as the third century B.C. in the Alexandrian poets.

Another passage in the *Argonautica* that seems to reflect the vistas of painting is that describing Eros' flight down from Olympus. He went out through (διέκ) the fruitful orchard of the palace of Zeus, and then he went out (ἐξήλυθεν) the airy gates of Olympus. From there (ἔνθεν) downward (καταιβάτις) was his heavenly path. Two poles held up (ἀνέχουσι) the peaks of steep (ἠλιβάτων) mountains, where the sun at its rising (ἀερθείς) reddens (ἐρεύθεται) with its first rays. Beneath (νειόθι) him now appeared the life-bearing earth and the cities of men, now the hilltops, and all around (ἀμφί) the sea, as he went through (ἀν') the vast air (III.158–66). We have here the sense of height and depth, of mist, air, and color, that we see in the Hellenistic wall-paintings, *skenographia* and perhaps in ἐρεύθεται *skiagraphia* as well, for that word, thematic in the *Argonautica*, obviously denotes a quality of light rather than a specific hue.[15]

Elsewhere too in Apollonius, the most painterly of the Hellenistic poets, we have combinations of *skenographia* and *skiagraphia;* in their exaggerated forms they produce a baroque effect. Book II, lines 164–77, is a brief example. The Argonauts after their victory over the Bebrycians spent the night drinking and feasting and singing to Orpheus' lyre, but

> when the sun rising from the distant lands lit the dewy hills (Ἦμος δ'ἠέλιος δροσερὰς ἐπέλαμψε κολώνας, / ἐκ περάτων ἀνιών) and roused the shepherds, then they loosed their hawsers from the trunk of the laurel and put on board all the spoil they needed to take and with the wind they steered through the swirling Bosporus (ἀνὰ Βόσπορον ἰθύνοντο). There a wave like a steep mountain rose up as though to rush upon them, ever lifted above the sails:[16]
>
> > ἔνθα μὲν ἠλιβάτῳἐναλίγκιον οὔρεϊ κῦμα
> > ἀμφέρεται προπάροιθεν ἐπαΐσσοντι † ἐοικός,
> > αἰὲν ὑπὲρ λαιφέων ἠερμένον.
>
> Nor would you say that they could escape, since it hangs (ἐπικρέμαται) furiously over the middle of the ship just like a cloud, but then it sinks (στόρνυται) altogether, if it meets with a good helmsman.

In these lines we have light breaking over dewy—that, is, glistening—hills; a sense of distance in the far-off hills, of recession into space from the Argonauts steering through the Bosporus; of great height and corresponding depth in the towering wave; of light and shade in the clouds.

The passage later in Book II (537–31) which tells of the Argonauts steering through the clashing rocks is filled with similar pictures, enhanced here by strong sound effects:

> > κοῖλαι δὲ σπήλυγγες ὑπὸ σπιλάδας τρηχείας
> > κλυζούσης ἁλὸς ἔνδον ἐβόμβεον, ὑψόθι δ'ὄχθης
> > λευκὴ καχλάζοντος ἀνέπτυε κύματος ἄχνη.
> >   (II.568–70)
>
> The hollow waves beneath the rough rocks thundered as the sea came surging in and the white foam of the splashing wave spurted high above the cliff.

Besides the onomatopoeia of κλυζούσης, ἐβόμβεον, καχλάζοντος, and ἀνέπτυε, we have in these lines strong alliteration in κ and σ and assonance in α and ο.

15. See Chapter 1.
16. Λαιφέων "sails" is Lloyd-Jones' emendation. The manuscripts read νεφέων (νεφέλων G) "clouds," which would be a still more dramatic contrast.

Another land and seascape in Book II (729–45) seems also to have been inspired by the art of painting. It too combines *skenographia, skiagraphia,* and sound. The Acherusian headland

rises up with steep crags, looking toward the Bithynian Sea. Beneath it bare rocks, washed by the sea, are rooted firm. Around them a rolling wave thunders loudly, but above, at its peak, spreading plane trees grow. From it there slopes gradually landward a hollow glade, where there is a cave of Hades roofed over by wood and rock. From here an icy breath, breathing continuously up from the chilling hollow, ever nourishes a shining white rime that melts in the midday sun. There is never silence there on that grim headland, but there is a constant murmur of the echoing sea and of the leaves that flutter in the winds from the cave. And here are the outpourings of the river Acheron which belches forth from the peak and falls into the eastern sea. A hollow ravine brings it down from above.

In this passage the prepositions, whether they stand alone or as prefixes, give perspective to the picture: ἀνίσχεται, εἰς, ὑπό, ἀμφί, ὕπερθεν, ἀμφιλαφεῖς, ἐκ, εἴσω, κατακέκλιται, ὕπαιθα, περιτέτροφε, κατά, διέξ, εἰς, κατάγει. The adverbs ἔνθεν and ἔνθα contribute too to the sense of space. In the height of the headland, the slope of the glade, the hollow of the cave, the outfall of the river from the cliff to the sea, we have *skenographia;* in the glistening of the rime, the midday sun, the quivering leaves, and the waterfall, *skiagraphia.*

Another passage that is remarkable for the sense of perspective is that describing the course of the river Thermodon:

> ἥ μέν τ' ἐξ ὀρέων κατανίσσεται ἤπειρόνδε
> ὑψηλῶν, ἅ τέ φασιν ᾿Αμαξόνια κλείεσθαι,
> ἔνθεν δ᾿αἰπυτέρην ἐπικίδναται ἔνδοθι γαῖαν
> ἀντικρύ· τῷ καί οἱ ἐπίστροφοί εἰσι κέλευθοι,
> ἀιεὶ δ᾿ ἄλλυδις ἄλλη, ὅπη κύρσειε μάλιστα
> ἠπείρου χθαμαλῆς, εἰλίσσεται, ἥ μὲν ἄπωθεν,
> ἥ δὲ πέλας πολέες δὲ πόροι νώνυμνοι ἔασιν
> ὅππη ὑπεξαφύονται, ὁ δ' ἀμφαδὸν ἄμμιγα παύροις
> Πόντον ἐς ῎Αξεινον κυρτὴν ὑπ' ἐρεύγεται ἄκρην.
>
> (II.976–84)

This flows down to the plain from the lofty mountains which they say are called the Amazonians. From there it spreads inland over steep country straight on. Its streams are winding. One runs forever this way, another that, wherever they may best seek lower ground, one far off, another close by. Many streams are drained off and go without a name. But mingled with a few the Thermodon openly spews its arching peak into the Inhospitable Pontus.

Here is the same remarkable use of prepositions and adverbs together with words actually denoting the winding of the main river and its many streams from the mountains down to the sea to create a sense of height and distance but more especially a sense of depth or recession into space. It is *skenographia* in words.

These city, land, and sea scapes in Callimachus and Apollonius anticipate Strabo's description of the Campus Martius (V.3.8) with its implied definition of *skenographia:*

καὶ τὰ περικείμενα ἔργα καὶ τὸ ἔδαφος ποάζον
δι᾽ ἔτους καὶ τῶν λόφων στεφάναι τῶν ὑπὲρ τοῦ
ποταμοῦ μέχρι τοῦ ῥείθρου σκηνογραφικὴν ὄψιν
ἐπιδεικνύμεναι δυσπάλλακτον παρέχουσι τὴν θέαν.

And the works of art which lie round about and the ground which is covered with grass all the year round, and the crowns of the hills—which above the river, as far up as its channel, present to the view a scene painting—offer a spectacle from which it is difficult to move away.

The creation of a third dimension was a concern of Hellenistic sculptors and architects as well as of the painters. *Skenographia* was related to optics, and optics played a part in the attempt of these artists to conquer space. Sculptors and architects alike had to compensate for the distortions of the eye. Heron (*Definitions* CXXXV.13) states this clearly: "The skenographia part of optics seeks [to discover] how one ought to paint [or draw] images of buildings. For since things do not appear such as they in fact are, they look to see not how they will reveal the underlying shapes, but rather, they render them in whatever way they appear. The end of the architect is to make his work shapely in appearance, and so far as it is possible, to find remedies for the deceptions of the vision, aiming not at balance or shapeliness based on truth [or reality] but at these as they appear to the vision."

It is dangerous to make generalizations about the progress of sculpture during the Hellenistic period. Classicizing and archaizing appear to contradict the steady striving toward realism that one expects from a study of earlier periods.[17] One or two observations may be made, however. During the first two centuries at least, in the periods of Early and High Hellenistic art, there was a tendency toward triangular composition in sculpture. At the same time there was a progression toward more open composition.[18] A part of the former is the increased torsion in bodies; of the latter, an ability to make figures with limbs flung in all directions. Both of these were apt to result in greater realism. The third dimension that artists achieved engaged the spectator in a way that archaic and even classical sculpture had not. The Crouching Aphrodite, the original of which dated to 250–240 B.C., is a splendid example (fig. 97). The twist of her body, the resulting folds of her flesh, and the very angle of her

17. Havelock, *HA* 113.
18. Ibid. 115–16.

122. Dancing maiden, Museum of Fine
Arts, Budapest

head, which looks over her shoulder, tempt one to walk around her body. The generally triangular shape of the sculpture is obvious. The statuette of a dancing maiden in the Museum of Fine Arts, Budapest, which dates to the first half of the third century B.C., is an exaggerated example of the same technique (fig. 122). The young woman twists her body until her shoulders are almost at right angles with her feet. Her mantle, held up before her by her concealed right hand, swirls in heavy folds around her. Some of its folds are

123. Dancing satyr, Museo
Nazionale, Naples

entirely horizontal. The composition is closed, the movement directed inward,
the whole again, from whatever angle, triangular. The swirling motion of the
dancer engages the spectator, takes him with her through all three dimensions.
The dancing satyr and the satyr falling asleep (figs. 123 and 124), in the
Museo Nazionale in Naples, Roman copies of Greek originals of a slightly
later period (200–150 B.C.), are extraordinary examples of open composition.
The abandon of the limbs is remarkable. The satyr dances on his toes, twists

124. Satyr falling asleep, Museo
Nazionale, Naples

his torso, and balances himself with his arms, one flung to the side, the other
held almost straight up before him. Clearly he fills three dimensions. The
other, seated satyr almost sprawls on his rock. His legs are spread, his left arm
hangs heavily at his side while he casts his right wearily over his tipped-back
head. The composition is both open and triangular. The back slant of his torso
draws the spectator toward him, engages him, as does the twist of the dancing
satyr's body, in a manner that earlier, more quadrilateral statues could not.

Architects of the Hellenistic period also worked with a new sense of
the third dimension. As Onians puts it, they turned void into space.[19] In the
laying out or rebuilding of cities they often abandoned internal symmetry of
individual buildings in favor of the perspective of a spectator entering an
entire complex of buildings. Here again the science of optics came to the fore.
The architect sought a larger symmetry on the visual axis. Onians believes
that this principle guided the plans of the second-century agoras of Miletus,
Magnesia-on-the-Meander, Priene, and Athens.[20] He describes too another,
smaller but equally interesting instance of the new concept of space: "In the

19. Onians 168.
20. Ibid. 169–75.

later Hellenistic period a garden was laid out around the temple of Hephaestus, above the Agora. Two rows of trees were set in holes along the sides and along the back of the building and these trees were aligned exactly on the columns of the temple so that the geometrical organization of the fifth-century structure was extended into the surrounding environment. The real colonnade of the temple is surrounded by what amounts to a double colonnade of trees, which immediately integrates the architecture with the surrounding space." [21] All this is a way of engaging the spectator. It is comparable to what the sculptors were achieving in their three-dimensional compositions. It came about, as Onians has correctly seen, from a new view, fostered by the science of optics, of space. [22]

The conquest of space in painting and sculpture led to a greater realism, which was reflected in the poetry of the period. The detailed psychological portrait of Medea, in love and remorse, in the *Argonautica* is comparable in realism to the expressions on the faces of Achilles and Briseis in the Pompeian wall painting copied from an original of about 300 B.C. (fig. 1). One reads in Achilles' face desire, pride, anger, and hurt. Briseis' stance is modest, her expression deliberately enigmatic. It seems, however, to combine shyness and anger. And yet, the best of Hellenistic poetry and art goes beyond realism. Once these painters and sculptors had mastered the third, they were able to achieve a fourth, even a fifth dimension. The quality that accounts for this is what the ancient art and literary critics called *phantasia*, "imagination" or "inspiration."

The crucial definition of *phantasia* comes in Aristotle (*De Anima* 428a ff.) It is a faculty of the soul which retains images. It is independent of opinion or rational thought. It is separate from but dependent upon αἴσθησις "sense perception," for αἴσθησις, a form of κίνησις "movement," sets it in motion.

From Philostratus (*VA* VI.19) we have the story of Apollonius of Tyana, who declared that Phidias and Praxiteles did not go up to heaven and make copies of the gods and then return to earth to represent them in their art. Rather, they were guided by a thing full of wisdom, namely *phantasia*, "a craftsman much wiser than imitation. For imitation will represent that which it has seen but phantasia that which it has not seen, for it will assume reality as its base."

Philostratus the Younger (Ἐικόνες proem. 5–6) in discussing *symmetria* in painting implies that it takes more than this (to create art) and then makes a remark which links the poetic and the visual arts: One who looks into this finds that "the art [of painting] has a certain kinship with poetry and that there is a certain imagination (φαντασία) which is common to both." In painting we see this suprarealism in copies of second-century B.C. landscapes: the pas-

21. Ibid. 168.
22. Ibid. 175–78.

toral scene with man and ram (fig. 76) and the landscape of the Abduction of Hylas (fig. 20). In the former we have perspective, but the pink rocks piled behind the monument are stacked unrealistically, and the light that illuminates the whole has an eerie quality. Here color—mauve, pink, blues, greens, and rusts—as well as *skiagraphia* and *skenographia* are made magic by that extra quality, *phantasia*. The same can be said of the Hylas landscape, where the dark blues, mauve, pink, and rust colors are shot through with an almost supernatural light. In the Odyssey frieze too the landscape with the Laestrygonians has in its swaying trees and pastel colors a dreamlike quality that can again be called *phantasia* (fig. 77). Another painting that has a particularly fantastic quality is that of Dionysus discovering the sleeping Ariadne (fig. 125). The original of this also dated to the second century B.C. The scene is set at dawn, and the figures are seen in a delicate light that penetrates the morning mist swirling behind them. Here surely is *skiagraphia* at its best. Highlights and shadows are cast in almost every tint and shade of the rainbow: pale greens, pinks, mauves, brown, gold, and ivory in Dionysus himself and his clothing, and in the flesh of an unearthly Pan, who, standing behind him with his hand raised in astonishment, is of a grayish mauve that complements his somewhat sinister face. The expression on Dionysus' face as he catches sight of Ariadne's naked body is also delicately done. He looks as though he himself believes that he has been caught in this dream that is a painting. It goes beyond the portrayal of ἦθος and πάθος—character and emotion—which the painter of Achilles and Briseis had achieved (fig. 1); that is, it goes beyond imitation to *phantasia*.[23]

So too in sculpture, the faces of the gods, the giants, the beasts, and the snakes of the Pergamene sculptures go beyond the expression of ἦθος and πάθος, of the merely human. They surpass the realism of the portraits of the early Hellenistic period—of Demosthenes, for instance (fig. 4)—and achieve the suprareal. Of course, archaic and classical sculpture had also been able to give the effect of portraying "the pattern laid up in heaven," but these baroque reliefs portray not serenity but passion. Still, even in the most passionately expressive faces there is unmistakable godhead. This is true of the beasts as well as the giants, of the "Biter" as well as of the lovely Nyx (figs. 126–127). It is true too of the stylized snakes. Nowhere else is *phantasia* so magnificently achieved.

These fantastic effects occurred in literature almost a century earlier than in the works of painting and sculpture cited above. We have, however, lost so much of both the literature and the art—and of course almost all original painting—that it is not at all safe to suggest a chronology; the poets may have inspired the artists, or the artists may have inspired the poets. It is more likely

23. On *ethos* and *pathos* see Pollitt, *The Ancient View* 184–89.

125. Dionysus discovers the sleeping Ariadne, Museo Nazionale, Naples

182

that the development was more or less contemporaneous and the inspiration mutual.

Phantasia is surely responsible for some of the more memorable of Theocritus' *Idylls*: for VI and XI, with their combination of the grotesque, the burlesque, and the pathetic in the portrait of the Cyclops in love; in the lush ending of VII, with its paradisaical description of the fruits of the "harvest home." These are all suprareal. It is in Apollonius, however, that we have the most gorgeous and baroque passages, comparable in *phantasia* to the Ariadne painting or the Pergamene sculptures. One of the loveliest of these is the description in *Argonautica* IV.930ff. of the Nereids passing the Argo from hand to hand over the wandering rocks.[24] They were like dolphins that in fair weather leap up from the depths and to the delight of sailors sport about the ship. They lifted their dresses above their snow-white knees, and up on the very rocks where the waves broke they rushed along on this side and on that. They were like girls on a sandy beach who roll their dresses up to their waists and play with a rounded ball. They catch it, one from another, and toss it high in the air and it never touches the ground. So did they in turn send the ship one from another through the air and over the waves, as it sped ever away from the rocks. Around them the water spouted and seethed. For so long as a day is lengthened in the spring of the year, so long did they labor, heaving the ship between the echoing rocks. And when they had fulfilled the commands of the wife of Zeus, they plunged like sea-mews into the depths.

Another passage from *Argonautica*, IV.1280ff., gives a different but equally magical effect. The Argonauts were grounded at the Syrtes, and in their despair their hearts grew numb and a pallor spread over their cheeks.

> They were like lifeless specters who wander through a city awaiting the outcome of war or plague or some unspeakable storm that washes over the myriad labors of oxen, when statues of their own accord sweat and run with blood and bellowings are heard (φαντάζωνται) in temples, or when the sun in the middle of the day draws on night from the heaven, and the stars shine bright through the mist. . . . They wrapped their heads in their cloaks and, fasting, lay down all that night and the next day, awaiting a pitiable death. Apart from these, the maidens huddled and lamented as when, forsaken, unfledged nestlings fallen from a cleft in the rock cheep shrilly, or when by the banks of the beautifully flowing Pactolus swans raise their song and all around the dewy meadow sounds and the river's lovely streams; so they, laying in the dust their yellow hair, grieved piteously all the night long.

Here are two paintings of despair, one ghostly, the other pathetic. In the former

---

24. Körte, *Hellenistic Poetry* 236, also saw this passage as a superb example of the baroque: "The plastic charm of this scene and its great effectiveness, fitted as it is with all the trappings of baroque art, are on a level hardly reached again in Apollonius' poem. Here the gods have the same grandeur as on the frieze of the altar at Pergamum."

126. "The Biter," from the frieze of the Great Altar of Zeus at Pergamum, Staatliches Museum, East Berlin

127. Nyx from the frieze of the Great Altar of Zeus at Pergamum, Staatliches Museum, East Berlin

there is an uncanny light, not unlike that in the Hylas landscape (fig. 20). In both, the figures lying on the ground in the night have spatial reality, the men with their heads wrapped in their cloaks, the young women with their blond hair spread in the dust. Again, this is more than realism. It is *phantasia*, the very word Apollonius himself uses, in verbal form, in line 1285 to denote the "appearance"—that is, the "sound"—of the μυκαί "bellowing" of cattle.

Conclusion

Hellenistic poetry and art alike are characterized by a great variety of subject, mood, and technique. They treat goddesses and hunchbacks, babies and crones, nutshells and octopi. They present the sweet passion of the princess Medea and the grotesquerie of the Cyclops in love. They work in epigram, epic, hymn, and pastoral; in bronze, marble, and terra-cotta sculpture; in silver and gold jewelry and tableware; in mosaic and wall paintings. Styles include the baroque, classicizing, and archaizing. One can point to a number of factors which may have contributed to this splendor of offerings. The conquests of Alexander surely stimulated a passion for the exotic. The mixed population of his city and of the other capitals of the Hellenistic world must also have produced a tolerance for difference.[1] The medical school and even the zoo at Alexandria certainly account in part for the passion for accuracy and detail in the presentation of the so-called grotesques and the exotic creatures of, for instance, the Nilotic mosaics. Epicureanism may have helped shape the pastoral,[2] and Stoicism the pathetic fallacy, and both may account for the new interest in the particular. What seems most of all, however, to govern the Hellenistic aesthetic is a *joie de vivre,* resulting perhaps from an expanded prosperity, but more likely from the exhilaration arising from the very variety of peoples and cultures which it in turn tried to represent. One must not

1. For a discussion of the population of Alexandria during the Hellenistic period see Fraser, *Ptolemaic Alexandria* I, 38–92.
2. T. G. Rosenmeyer, *The Green Cabinet: Theocritus and the European Pastoral Lyric* (Berkeley, 1969) 11–12 and passim; S. F. Walker, *Theocritus* 22–24. Cf., however, G. Lawall, *Theocritus' Coan Pastorals* (Cambridge, Mass., 1967) 117.

forget, either, the natural beauty of Alexandria's setting nor the constructed beauty of that extraordinary city.[3] So these poets and artists took joy in the tentacles of the octopus, the teeth of the rhinoceros, the legs of the cicada; in the vertebrae of the hunchback as well as in the folds of Aphrodite's flesh. They delighted in black street musicians, drunken old women, dying Persians and Gauls, sleeping satyrs, and dancing dwarfs. Nothing was too ugly or too sad for their attention. Their passion was for the particulars of life, and these they represented with realism and with magic.

3. Our earliest descriptions of the city are in Strabo XVII and, from the third century A.D., in Achilles Tatius' novel *Leucippe and Cleitophon* (V.1.2). The latter describes two main streets, intersecting at right angles and running through the city from one end to the other. Cleitophon saw, he says, countless rows of columns in whatever direction he turned. He also described the entire city as being illuminated at night. "It was," he claimed, "as if another sun had risen that spread its rays in every direction. I saw there a city whose beauty rivalled that of the heavens."

Epilogue

Alexandria today is a shabby city. Pavements are badly cracked. Paint peels and plaster crumbles from the once elegant apartment houses along the Corniche. Even the palms are pathetic. The city is almost entirely Arabic-speaking, for the Greek and other foreign communities have vanished. Most visitors are bitterly disappointed. And yet, on the third floor of the Greek Embassy there are the books, a good classical collection; the furniture, delicately inlaid with mother-of-pearl and upholstered in red velvet; the photographs, manuscripts, and death mask of the poet Cavafy. On Tatwig Street one encounters still the halt and the blind that surrounded Scobie, that scoundrel of Lawrence Durrell's invention. Indeed, these two, Cavafy and Durrell, preserve to a remarkable degree the spirit of ancient Alexandria.

One of the most pervasive themes in the poetry of Cavafy is that of the city, ancient and modern; he seems not entirely to distinguish between the two. When he steps out on his own balcony to see a little of the city he loves, "a little movement on the street, and in the shops,"[1] he seems to remember the ancient city as well as to take comfort from the modern, for he has been reading and rereading a love letter and remembering the sensuality of his youth:

> But how potent were the perfumes,
> on how splendid a bed we lay,
> to what sensual delight we gave our bodies.
> > "In the Evening"

These are the themes, this is the mood in which he writes of the lovers of antiquity.

---

1. The translations of Cavafy I cite are those of Rae Dalven, *The Complete Poems of Cavafy* (New York, 1961).

Apart from the love poems, however, the poet evokes the splendor of the ancient city itself. In "The Glory of the Ptolemies," Lagus, who is Ptolemy I Soter, speaks of "The city—the teacher, summit of panhellenism, in the word, in every art, the wisest." Cavafy here dwells upon the learning of the city. In "The God Forsakes Antony," he recreates the mystic quality of Alexandria when he bids Antony:

> As a last enjoyment listen to the sounds,
> the exquisite instruments of the mystical troupe,
> and bid her farewell, the Alexandria you are losing.

"In Alexandria, 31 B.C." reproduces something of the color and confusion which are common to the ancient and the modern city when the trader arrives "from his tiny village, close to the suburbs, and still covered with dust from the journey," and " 'Frankincense!' and 'Gum!', 'The Finest Olive Oil!' 'Scent for the Hair!' "

> He cries on the streets. But the great clamor of the mob,
> the medley of music and the parades, would they let
> > him be heard?

"The Sovereign from Western Libya," on the other hand, had to keep still, so afraid was he that he would speak "the Greek language with fearful barbarisms, and the Alexandrians would find him out, as is their habit, the horrible wretches."

"Of the Shop"—which tells of the jeweller wrapping in costly green silk "roses of ruby and lilies of pearl, and violets of amethyst," which were as he would have them and "not as he saw them in nature," and keeping them in his safe, "a sample of his intrepid and skilled craft"—might be about either the ancient or the modern city. The artistry of the jeweller is the link, for Cavafy when writing of either the ancient or the modern world emphasizes elegance and craft. "Dionysus and His Crew" is about the artisan Damon, who wants to go into politics. The "Sculptor of Tyana" displays his many statues but says that the one he loves best is the one he made on a warm summer day when his mind soared to the ideal, the one he dreamt of, the young Hermes. "Before the Statue of Endymion" endows that work of art with the same erotic attraction: "Now ecstatic I gaze at Endymion's illustrious beauty." The "Picture of a 23-Year-Old Youth Painted by His Friend of the Same Age, An Amateur" recalls the sensuousness of certain Hellenistic statues:

> open at the collar,   with a rose-colored shirt;
> also of the beauty   so something might be seen
> The right temple   of his chest, of his neck.
> covered by his hair,   is almost entirely
>   his beautiful hair

(parted in the manner	he prefers it this year).
There is the completely	voluptuous tone
he wanted to put into it	when he was doing the eyes,
when he was doing the lips . . .	His mouth, the lips
that are made for consummation,	for choice love-making.

Cavafy creates the sense of flesh that the Hellenistic poets, sculptors, and painters achieved. In "Artisan of Wine-Mixing Bowls" he again describes the craft of the Hellenistic artisan:

On this lovely wine-mixing bowl	of the purest silver—
. . . . . .	. . . . .
you see elegant flowers,	and brooks, and thyme,
and in the center I have placed	a young handsome man,
naked and amorous	one of his legs is still
plunged in the water.	

He writes here of sexuality as well as of skill.

Eroticism is perhaps the most obvious aspect of Cavafy's verse. The several poems entitled "Days of —" especially dwell upon the voluptuous joys of the flesh and so recall again the skill of the Hellenistic poets and artists in suggesting the same. "Days of 1901" tells of a young man of twenty-nine years who at rarest moments "gave the impression of a flesh almost untouched." In "Days of 1896" a young man of nearly thirty because of his erotic bent has lost his money and his reputation. He was a

genuine child of love	who unquestionably placed
higher than his honor,	and his reputation too,
the pure sensual delight	of his pure flesh.

In "Days of 1909, 1910, 1911" the poet asks himself if "in the days of antiquity glorious Alexandria possessed a more superb-looking youth." "Days of 1908" tells of poor youth who wore a shabby cinnamon-colored suit. When he cast off that and his mended underwear, "he remained entirely naked; flawlessly handsome, a marvel. His hair uncombed, standing up a little, his limbs somewhat tanned by the sun, by the morning nudity at the baths, at the beach." Again, this might well be a painting, a statue.

Other love poems are equally sensuous and evoke the same Alexandrian eroticism. In "At the Café Entrance" a young boy is described as a statue made by Eros "from his consummate experience":

> joyfully modelling its symmetrical limbs;
> heightening sculpturally its stature;
> modelling the face with emotion
> and imparting by the touch of his hands
> a feeling on the brow, on the eyes, on the lips.

In "One Night" the poet actually mentions the rosiness of flesh:

> I had the body of love, I had the lips,
> the voluptuous and rosy lips of ecstacy—.

Another description of a lover as a statue occurs in "So Much I Gazed":

> Contours of the body. Red lips. Voluptuous limbs.
> Hair as if taken from Greek statues. . . .

The sensuousness of Cavafy extends beyond the love poems to the epitaphs, which share in his eroticism. In "Beautiful Flowers and White That Became Him Well" we see the combination of love and death:

> On his very cheap coffin,   he placed flowers,
> beautiful flowers and white   that became him well,
> that became his beauty and   his twenty-two years.

This has some of the sensuality of the *Laments* for Bion and Adonis.

"The Grave of the Grammarian Lysias" and "The Grave of Eurion" are epitaphs quite in the Alexandrian manner. Lysias is buried with his "scholia, texts, grammars, scriptures, numerous commentaries in tomes on hellenisms." Eurion, a handsome Alexandrian boy of twenty-five years, was "a student of Aristocleitus in philosophy, of Paros in rhetoric. . . . He wrote a history of the province of Arsinoe. That at least will remain. But we have lost the most precious—his form, that was an Apollonian vision." "In Harbor" shares with Callimachus and other epigrammatists of the *Anthology* the pathos of the young man lost at sea. Just before he died he spoke of his home and his very old parents:

> But who they were nobody knew,
> nor which his country in the vast panhellenic world.
> It is better so. For in this way, though
> he lies dead in this little harbor,
> his parents will always go on hoping he is alive.

"Tomb of Iases" borrows the ancient conceit of having the dead man speak. His address to the wayfarer combines an ancient convention with a modern appraisal, probably quite correct, of the ancient city:

> Traveler,
> if you are an Alexandrian, you will not condemn,
> you know,
> the rushing torrent of our life; what ardor it has;
> what supreme pleasure.

Associated with the theme of young men dead is that of old men and the death of youth. These too are often treated quite sensuously. In "Very

Seldom" an old poet enters his door to hide "his wretchedness and his old age" and "meditates on the share he still has of youth":

> Now young people recite his verses.
> In their lively eyes his fancies pass.
> Their sound, voluptuous minds,
> their shapely, firm flesh
> are stirred by his expression of beauty.

"An Old Man" and "Candles" are purer pictures of old men regretting lost youth. "The Souls of Old Men" dwells upon the decaying flesh of old age:

> In their bodies wasted and aged
> sit the souls of old men.
>
> .   .   .   .   .   .
>
> souls, that sit—comicotragical—
> in their aged worn-out hides.

Here is the pathos of the old men—the slaves, pedagogues, shepherds, fishermen, philosophers—of Hellenistic sculpture and of the aged Phineus of Apollonius' *Argonautica*, who "rose from his couch like a lifeless dream and, bent over his staff, went to the door on wrinkled feet, touching the walls. As he moved his limbs trembled with weakness and age. His parched skin was squalid with dirt and only his hide held together his bones" (II.197–201). The sculptors were perhaps challenged by wrinkled skin, visible bone structure to display their technique. Cavafy, the epigrammatists of the *Anthology*, and Apollonius achieve similar effects with words.

Cavafy's interest in craft or technique is reflected in his poem "The Mirror in the Hall." A handsome lad, a tailor's employee, entered the hallway of a rich house. As he waited for his receipt, he looked at himself in "an enormous, extremely old mirror that must have been bought at least eighty years ago." That mirror had seen "Thousands of objects and faces . . ."

> but this time the mirror was delighted,
> and it felt proud that it had received unto itself
> for a few moments an image of flawless beauty.

Here, together with the theme of the poor but handsome youth, is that Hellenistic motif, the mirror.

Another Hellenistic motif, in addition to those of the city, love, youth, death, and sensuous beauty, is that of magic, which in Cavafy appears in his poem "According to the Ancient Formulas of Grecosyrian Magic." It too embraces the eroticism common to Cavafy and his Alexandrian predecessors. What witching herbs, he asks,

can evoke for me my twenty-three years;
can evoke again for me my friend
when he was twenty-two—his beauty, his love?

What extract can be found according to the formulas
prepared by the ancient Grecosyrian magi which,
along with this return to the past,
can also evoke for me our little room?

Lawrence Durrell was haunted by Cavafy, whom he refers to as the "old poet" and "the poet of the city," and, like Cavafy, by the memory of ancient Alexandria. He says of Justine: "She could not help but remind me of that race of terrific queens which left behind them the ammoniac smell of their incestuous loves to hover like a cloud over the Alexandrian subconscious. The giant man-eating cats like Arsinoe were her true siblings" (*Justine* 20).[2] His recall of the ancient city is deliberate: he was fully aware of the tradition in which he was working:

> As [Justine] speaks I am thinking of the founder of the city, the soldier-God in his glass coffin, the youthful body lapped in silver, riding down the river towards his tomb. . . . It is as if the preoccupations of this landscape were centred somewhere out of reach of the average inhabitant—in a region where the flesh, stripped by over-indulgence of its final reticences, must yield to a preoccupation vastly more comprehensive: or perish in a kind of exhaustion represented by the works of the Mouseion, the guileless play of hermaphrodites in the green courtyards of art and science. (*Justine* 39)

The hermaphrodite, a favorite subject in Hellenistic art, is a fitting symbol for what Durrell sees as the sexual variety of both the ancient and the modern city. This perception often underlies some of his most striking descriptions of the city:

> Five races, five languages, a dozen creeds: five fleets turning through their greasy reflections behind the harbour bar. But there are more than five sexes and only demotic Greek seems to distinguish among them. The sexual provender which lies to hand is staggering in its variety and profusion. You would never mistake it for a happy place. The symbolic lovers of the free Hellenic world are replaced here by something different, something subtly androgynous, inverted upon itself. The Orient cannot rejoice in the sweet anarchy of the body—for it has outstripped the body. I remember Nessim once saying—I think he was quoting —that Alexandria was the great wine-press of love; those who emerged from it were the sick men, the solitaries, the prophets—I mean all who have been deeply wounded in their sex. (*Justine* 14)

2. The page numbers for the quotations from *The Alexandria Quartet* are those of the Faber and Faber publication of 1957–60.

The mixture of populations and languages, the fleets in the harbor, the androgyny, are as descriptive of the ancient as of the modern city, and "all who have been deeply wounded in their sex" suggests the "sick men, the solitaries, the prophets" of Hellenistic as well as contemporary Alexandria.

Durrell is, like Apollonius, a painterly writer. His most memorable accounts of the city make stunning use of color terms. He uses too names from the artist's palette. Here, for instance, is a part of his first description of Alexandria: "Notes for landscape tones. . . . Long sequences of tempera. Light filtered through the essence of lemons. An air full of brick-dust—sweet-smelling brick-dust and the odour of hot pavements slaked with water. Light damp clouds, earth-bound, yet seldom bringing rain. Upon this squirt dust-red, dust-green, chalk-mauve and watered crimson-lake" (*Justine* 14). It is interesting, though probably coincidental, that these are the colors commonly found in the Alexandrian tomb-paintings.

Balthazar begins with another virtuoso description of colors: "Landscape tones: brown to bronze, steep skyline, low cloud, pearl ground with shadowed oyster and violet reflections. The lion-dust of desert: prophets' tombs turned to zinc and copper at sunset on the ancient lake. Its huge sand-faults like watermarks from the air; green and citron giving to gunmetal, to a single plum-dark sail, moist, palpitant: sticky-winged nymph. . . . Mareotis under a sky of hot lilac" (*Balthazar* 13). Here Durrell, like the Hellenistic poets and painters, plays with light and shade. He records not simply color but the changing of hues at sunset.

Elsewhere too Durrell creates such chiaroscuro effects. He speaks of the

> white city itself whose pearly skies are broken only by the white stalks of the minarets and the flocks of pigeons turning in clouds of silver and amethyst; whose viridian and black marble harbour-water reflects the snouts of foreign men-of-war turning through their slow arcs, depicting the prevailing wind; or swallowing their own inky reflections, touching and overlapping like the very tongues and sects and races over which they keep their uneasy patrol: symbolizing the western consciousness whose power is exemplified in steel—those sullen preaching guns against the yellow metal of the lake and the town which breaks open at sunset like a rose. (*Balthazar* 105)

The play of light upon the wheeling pigeons and upon the harbor waters is the sort of effect that the *skiagraphia* of the Hellenistic painters tried to achieve. Durrell himself once describes a mirage of the city as "luminous and trembling, as if painted on dusty silk" (*Balthazar* 16).

Durrell nowhere better displays his genius for creating painterly effects than he does in descriptions of birds. Here are ducks against a dawn sky: "Now rose-madder and warm burnt gold. Clouds move to green and yellow. . . . I see the black silhouette of teal cross my vision eastward" (*Justine* 214).

These pastel shades are those we find in the paintings of Achilles and Briseis and Dionysus Discovering the Sleeping Ariadne.

More dazzling still is this description of flamingoes: "suddenly the sky-line was sliced in half by a new flight, rising more slowly and dividing earth from air in a pink travelling wound; like the heart of a pomegranate staring through its skin. Then, turning from pink to scarlet, flushed back into white and fell to the lake-level like a shower of snow to melt as it touched the water —'Flamingo' they both cried and laughed, and the darkness snapped upon them, extinguishing the visible world" (*Mountolive* 13). This delight in color and light is reminiscent of but far surpasses Apollonius' best effects.

Durrell recalls the chiaroscuro of the Hellenistic painters and poets. He also recreates the mixture of populations and languages and the sexual variety of the ancient city. There is still another and equally remarkable way in which he echoes the Hellenistic Alexandria, and that is in his presentation of grotesques. Almost every single character in the four novels of *The Alexandria Quartet* is physically maimed as well as being "deeply wounded in his sex." Darley himself is lame. Hamid is one-eyed. Cohen is pock-marked. Melissa is dying of tuberculosis. Capodistria is extremely ugly: "He is more of a goblin than a man, you would think. The flat triangular head of the snake with the huge frontal lobes; the hair grows forward in a widow's peak. A whitish flickering tongue is forever busy keeping his thin lips moist" (*Justine* 33). More grotesque still is the barber Mnemjian, who is, like the ancient Alexandrian grotesques, both a dwarf and a hunchback. Panayatis has no tongue. Narouz has a harelip. Leila is pock-marked. Ali has had his ears cropped. Liza is blind. Leila's husband has a disease which atrophies the muscles. Scobie has a glass eye. Simla has no nose. Nessim loses one eye and a finger. Justine suffers a stroke which causes one eyelid to droop. Balthazar tries to cut off his hands. Abdul has lost an eye. Arif the musician is blind. Capodistria's Italian servants are deaf. Hamid's mother had put out both his brother's eyes. Clea loses a hand. And there are throughout incidental descriptions of grotesques. In *Balthazar*: "From the throat of a narrow alley . . . burst a long tilting gallery of human beings headed by the leaping acrobats and dwarfs of Alexandria" (155). In *Clea* at the procession along Tatwig Street in the festival for El Scob: "First came the grotesque acrobats and tumblers with masks and painted faces, rolling and contorting, leaping the air and walking on their hands," and "Showal the dwarf was teasing them from his booth at ground level and causing screams of laughter at his well-aimed arrows. He had a high tinny little voice and the most engaging of acrobatic tricks despite his stunted size. He talked continuously even when standing on his head, and punctuated the point of his patter with a double somersault. His face was grotesquely farded and his lips painted in a clown's grin" (260).

The mutilated characters of the narrative—Balthazar, Clea, Liza, Leila—

are like those ancient grotesques which seem to be representations of actual pathological conditions—Pott's Disease, chondrodystrophic dwarfism—but these dwarfs and acrobats more closely resemble the joyful dancing dwarfs from the Tunisian shipwreck and the comical grotesques in the Fouquet Collection. Scobie and Mnemjian partake of both the pathos of the former and the humor and obscenity of the latter. They are perhaps the characters which provide the strongest link to that ancient Alexandria which haunts the city that Cavafy knew, that Durrell invented, that both of them loved.

WORKS CITED

SOURCES FOR ILLUSTRATIONS

INDEX

Works Cited

Barkhuizen, J. H. "The Psychological Characterization of Medea in Apollonius of Rhodes, *Argonautica* 3, 744–824." *Acta Classica* 22 (1979) 33–48.

Bayer, E. *Fischerbilder in der hellenistischen Plastik.* Bonn, 1983.

Becatti, G. "Lo stile arcaistico." *La Critica d'Arte: Rivista Bimestrale di Arti Figurative per il Mondo Antico* 6 (1941) 32–48.

Beye, C. R. "Jason as Love-Hero in Apollonius' *Argonautica.*" *Greek, Roman, and Byzantine Studies 10* (1969) 31–55.

Bieber, M. *The Sculpture of the Hellenistic Age.* New York, 1961.

Binsfield, W. *Grylloi.* Cologne, 1956.

Blanckenhagen, P. H. von. "The Odyssey Frieze." *Mitteilungen des deutschen archäologischen Instituts, Römische Abteilung* 70 (1963) 100–137.

Blanckenhagen, P. H. von, and Alexander, C. *The Paintings of Boscoreale.* Heidelberg, 1962.

Bogue, P. L. P. "Astronomy in the *Argonautica* of Apollonius Rhodius." Dissertation, University of Illinois, Urbana, 1977.

Brown, B. R. *Ptolemaic Paintings and Mosaics and the Alexandrian Style.* Cambridge, Mass., 1957.

Bruno, V. J. *Form and Color in Greek Painting.* New York, 1977.

Buller, J. L. "The Pathetic Fallacy in Hellenistic Pastoral." *Ramus* 10 (1981) 35–52.

Bulloch, A. W. "A Callimachean Refinement to the Greek Hexameter." *Classical Quarterly* 20 (1970) 258–68.

Bulloch, A. W. "Apollonius Rhodius *Argonautica* 2, 177: A Case-Study in Hellenistic Poetic Style." *Hermes* 101 (1973) 496–98.

Capovilla, G. "Nuovi contributi a Callimaco." *Studi Italiani di Filologia Classica* 42 (1970) 94–153.

Carpenter, R. *Greek Sculpture*. Chicago, 1960.

Carspecker, J. F. "Apollonius Rhodius and the Homeric Epic." *Yale Classical Studies* 13 (1952) 33–143.

Cavafy, C. *The Complete Poems of Cavafy*. Translated by Rae Dalven. New York, 1961.

Charbonneaux, J.; Martin, R.; and Villard, F. *Hellenistic Art, 330–50 B.C.* London, 1973.

Citti, V. "Lettura di Arato." *Vichiana* 2 (1965) 146–70.

Clark, R. J. "A Note on Medea's Plant and the Mandrake." *Folklore* 79 (1968) 227–31.

Couat, A. *Alexandrian Poetry under the First Three Ptolemies, 324–222 B.C.* Translated by J. Loeb. London, 1931.

Coulton, J. J. *Ancient Greek Architects at Work*. Ithaca, N.Y., 1977.

Cunningham, I. C. *Herodas, Mimiambi*. Oxford, 1971.

Deubner, L. *Attische Feste*. Berlin, 1932.

Dinesen, I. *Out of Africa*. New York, 1937; reprinted, 1972.

Dodds, E. R. *The Greeks and the Irrational*. Berkeley and Los Angeles, 1951.

Durrell, L. *Justine*. London, 1957.

Durrell, L. *Balthazar*. London, 1958.

Durrell, L. *Mountolive*. London, 1958.

Durrell, L. *Clea*. London, 1960.

Effe, B. "Προτέρη γενεή: Eine stoische Hesiod-interpretation in Arats *Phainomena*." *Rheinisches Museum für Philologie* 113 (1970) 167–82.

Elvira, M. A. "Apolonio de Rodas y la pintura del primer helenismo." *Archivo Español de Arquelogía* 50–51 (1977–78) 33–46.

Ferguson, J. "The Epigrams of Callimachus." *Greece and Rome* 17 (1970) 64–80.

Fitzgerald, R. *Odyssey*. New York, 1963.

Fowler, B. H. "Lyric Structures in Three Euripidean Plays." *Dioniso* 49 (1978) 15–51.

Fowler, B. H. "The Centaur's Smile: Pindar and the Archaic Aesthetic." In *Ancient Greek Art and Iconography*, edited by Warren G. Moon, 159–70. Madison, 1983.

Fowler, B. H. "The Archaic Aesthetic." *American Journal of Philology* 105 (1984) 119–49.

Fränkel, H. *Apollonii Rhodii Argonautica*. Oxford, 1961; reprinted, 1964, 1967.

Fraser, P. M. *Ptolemaic Alexandria*. Vols. 1–3. Oxford, 1972.

Fuchs, W. *Die Dornauszieher*. Opus Nobile 8. Bremen, 1958.

Fuchs, W. *Die Vorbilder der neuattischen Reliefs: Jahrbuch des Deutschen Archäologischen Instituts*. Erganzungsheft 20 (1959).

Garson, R. W. "Homeric Echoes in Apollonius Rhodius' *Argonautica*." *Classical Philology* 67 (1972) 1–9.

Giangrande, G. *Zu Sprachgebrauch, Technik und Text des Apollonius Rhodios, Class. and Byz. Monogr. I*. Amsterdam, 1973.

Gillies, M. M. "The Ball of Eros." *Classical Review* 38 (1924) 50–51.

Gold, L. H. "Adjectives in Theocritus: A Study of Poetic Diction in the Pastoral Idylls." Dissertation, University of Wisconsin, Madison, 1976.

Gow, A.S.F. *Bucolici Graeci*. Oxford, 1952; reprinted 1962, 1966.

Gow, A.S.F. *Theocritus*. 2 vols. Cambridge, 1965.

Gow, A.S.F., and Page, D. L. *The Greek Anthology: Hellenistic Epigrams*. 2 vols. Cambridge, 1965.

Gutzwiller, K. J. "The Hellenistic Epyllion: A Literary Examination." Dissertation, University of Wisconsin, Madison, 1977.

Gutzwiller, K. J. "Studies in the Hellenistic Epyllion." *Beiträge zur klassischen Philologie* 114 (1981) 1–95.

Gutzwiller, K. J. "The Plant Decoration on Theocritus' Ivy Cup." *American Journal of Philology* 107 (1986) 253–55.

Halperin, D. M. *Before Pastoral: Theocritus and the Ancient Tradition of Bucolic Poetry*. New Haven, 1983.

Hanfmann, G.M.A. "Hellenistic Art." *Dumbarton Oaks Papers* 17 (1963) 77–94.

Harrison, E. B. *Archaic and Archaistic Sculpture: The Athenian Agora XI*. Princeton, 1965.

Havelock, C. M. "Archaistic Reliefs of the Hellenistic Period." *American Journal of Archaeology* 68 (1964) 43–58.

Havelock, C. M. "The Archaic as Survival versus the Archaistic as a New Style." *American Journal of Archaeology* 69 (1965) 331–40.

Havelock, C. M. *Hellenistic Art*. Greenwich, Conn., 1971; 2nd edition, New York, 1981.

Headlam, W. and Knox, A. D. *Herodas*. Cambridge, 1922.

Herter, H. "Kallimachos und Homer." In *Kleine Schriften*, 378–79. Munich, 1975.

Himmelmann, N. *Alexandria und der Realismus in der griechischen Kunst*. Tübingen, 1983.

Hoffman, H., and Davidson, P. *Greek Gold: Jewelry from the Age of Alexander*. Boston, Museum of Fine Arts; New York, Brooklyn Museum; Richmond, Virginia Museum of Fine Arts, 1966.

Hurst, A. *Apollonios de Rhodes, manière et cohérence: Contribution a l'étude de l'esthétique alexandrine*. Bibl. Helvetica Rom. VIII. Berne, 1967.

James, A. W. "Some Examples of Imitation in the Similes of Later Greek Epic." *Antichthon* 3 (1969) 77-90.

James, A. W. "The Zeus Hymns of Cleanthes and Aratus." *Antichthon* 6 (1972) 28–38.

Keuls, E. "Skiagraphia Once Again." *American Journal of Archaeology* 79 (1975) 1–16.

Kidd, D. A. "The Fame of Aratus." *AUMLA* (1961) no. 15, 5–18. *Journal of The Australasian Universities Language and Literature Association*

Klein, W. *Vom antiken Rokoko*. Vienna, 1921.

Körte, A. *Hellenistic Poetry*. Translated by J. Hammer and M. Hadas. New York, 1929.

Laubscher, H. P. *Fischer und Landleute: Studien zur hellenistischen Genreplastik.* Mainz am Rhein, 1982.

Lawall, G. "Simaetha's Incantation: Structure and Imagery." *Transactions of the American Philological Association* 92 (1961) 283–94.

Lawall, G. "Apollonius' *Argonautica*: Jason as Anti-Hero." *Yale Classical Studies* 19 (1966) 119–69.

Lawall, G. *Theocritus' Coan Pastorals.* Cambridge, Mass., 1967.

Lehmann, P. W. *Roman Wall Painting from Boscoreale in the Metropolitan Museum of Art.* Cambridge, Mass., 1953.

Lendle, O. "Die Spiegelkugel des Zeus (Apoll. Rhod. *Arg.* 3, 137–140)." *Hermes* 107 (1979) 493–95.

Levi, D. "The Evil Eye and the Lucky Hunchback." *Antioch-on-the-Orontes* 3 (Princeton, 1941) 220–32.

Levine, D. N. "Δίπλαξ πορφυρέη." *Rivista di Filologia e di Istruzione Classica* 98 (1970) 17–36.

Ling, R. "Hylas in Pompeian Art." *Mélanges d'Archéologie et d'Histoire de l'Ecole Française de Rome* 91 (1979) 773–816.

Long, A. A. *Hellenistic Philosophy.* London, 1974.

Luck, G. "Aratea." *American Journal of Philology* 97 (1976) 213–34.

Ludwig, W. "Die *Phainomena* Arats als hellenistische Dichtung." *Hermes* 91 (1963) 425–48.

McKay, K. J. *The Poet at Play: Kallimachos, The Bath of Pallas.* Supplement VI to *Mnemosyne.* Leiden, 1962.

McKay, K. J. *Erysichthon: A Callimachean Comedy.* Supplement VII to *Mnemosyne.* Leiden, 1962.

McKay, K. J. "Mischief in Kallimachos' *Hymn to Artemis*." *Mnemosyne* 16 (1963) 243–56.

Mair, A. W. *Aratus.* Loeb Classical Library. London and Cambridge, Mass., 1921; revised and reprinted, 1955, 1960.

Mitchell, C. "Stylistic Problems in Greek and Roman Archaistic Reliefs." *Harvard Studies in Classical Philology* 61 (1953) 73–84.

Mooney, G. W. *Apollonius Rhodius, Argonautica.* Dublin, 1912; reprinted, Amsterdam, 1964.

Newman, J. K. *The Classical Epic Tradition.* Madison, 1986.

Nicosia, S. *Teocrito e l'arte figurata.* Quad. dell' Ist. di Filol. greca della Univ. di Palermo V. Palermo, 1968.

Oliver, A., Jr. *Silver for the Gods: Eight Hundred Years of Greek and Roman Silver.* Toledo, Museum of Art, 1977.

Onians, J. *Art and Thought in the Hellenistic Age.* London, 1979.

Oppermann, H. "Herophilos bei Kallimachos." *Hermes* 60 (1925) 14–32.

Pemberton, E. "A Note on Skiagraphia." *American Journal of Archaeology* 80 (1976) 82–84.

Perdrizet, P. *Les terres cuites grecques d'Egypte de la Collection Fouquet.* Paris, 1921.

Pfeiffer, R. *Callimachus.* 2 vols. Oxford, 1949; reprinted, 1965.

Phinney, E., Jr. "Hellenistic Painting and the Poetic Style of Apollonius." *Classical Journal* 62 (1966–67) 145–49.

Phinney, E., Jr. "Narrative Unity in the *Argonautica*: The Medea-Jason Romance." *Transactions of the American Philological Association* 98 (1967) 327–41.

Phillips, K. "The Barberini Mosaic." Dissertation, Princeton University, 1962.

Pokorny, J. *Indogermanisches etymologisches Wörterbuch.* 2 vols. Bern and Munich, 1959.

Pollitt, J. J. *The Ancient View of Greek Art.* New Haven and London, 1974.

Pollitt, J. J. *Art in the Hellenistic Age.* Cambridge, 1986.

Rice, E. E. *The Grand Procession of Ptolemy Philadelphus.* Oxford, 1983.

Rosenmeyer, T. G. *The Green Cabinet: Theocritus and the European Pastoral Lyric.* Berkeley, 1969.

Sale, W. "The Popularity of Aratus." *Classical Journal* 61 (1965) 160–64.

Schmidt, E. *Archaistische Kunst in Griechenland und Rom.* Munich, 1922.

Schmidt, R. *Die Darstellung von Kinderspielzeug und Kinderspiel in der griechischen Kunst.* Vienna, 1977.

Schwabl, H. "Zur Mimesis bei Arat: Prooimion und Parthenos." In *Antidosis: Festschrift für Walter Kraus zum 70. Geburtstag*, edited by R. Hanslik, A. Lesky, and H. Schwabl. Vienna, 1972.

Segal, C. *Poetry and Myth in Ancient Pastoral.* Princeton, 1981.

Shapiro, H. A. "Notes on Greek Dwarfs." *American Journal of Archaeology* 88 (1984) 391–92.

Shumacher, J. W. "Homeric Transformations in the *Argonautica* of Apollonius of Rhodes." Dissertation, University of Pennsylvania, 1969.

Snell, B. *The Discovery of the Mind.* Translated by T. G. Rosenmeyer. Cambridge, Mass., 1953.

Snowden, F. *Blacks in Antiquity: Ethiopians in the Greco-Roman Experience.* Cambridge, Mass., 1970.

Solmsen, F. "Greek Philosophy and the Discovery of the Nerves." *Museum Helveticum* 18 (1961) 169–97.

Stanford, W. B. *Greek Metaphor.* Oxford, 1936.

Stevenson, W. E. III. "The Pathological Grotesque Representation in Greek and Roman Art." Dissertation, University of Pennsylvania, 1975.

Swindler, M. H. *Ancient Painting.* New Haven, 1929.

Trypanis, C. A. "The Character of Alexandrian Poetry." *Greece and Rome* 16 (1947) 6–7.

Trypanis, C. A. *Callimachus.* Loeb Classical Library. Cambridge, Mass., and London, 1958.

Ver Ecke, P. *Euclide, L'Optique et la Catoptrique.* Paris, 1959.

Walker, S. F. *Theocritus*. Boston, 1980.

Webster, T. B. L. *Hellenistic Poetry and Art*. London, 1964.

White, J. D. *Perspective in Ancient Drawing and Painting*. Society for the Promotion of Hellenic Studies, Supplementary Paper no. 7. London, 1956.

Wilamowitz, U. von. *Hellenistische Dichtung*. 2 vols. Berlin, 1924.

Yalouris, N.; Andronikos, M.; Rhompiopoulou, K.; Hermann, A.; and Vermeule, C. *The Search for Alexander*. New York Graphic Society, with the cooperation of the Greek Ministry of Culture and Sciences. Boston, 1980.

Zahn, R. *Ausstellung von Schmuckarbeiten aus Edelmetall aus den Staatlichen Museen zu Berlin*. Berlin, 1932.

Zanker, G. *Realism in Alexandrian Poetry: A Literature and Its Audience*. London; Sydney; Wolfeboro, N.H., 1987.

Sources for Illustrations

Acknowledgment is made to the sources listed below for reproduction of the illustrations.

1. Museo Nazionale, Naples
2. Trustees of the British Museum, London
3. Palazzo Grazioli, Rome
4. Ny Carlsberg Glyptotek, Copenhagen
5. Trustees of the British Museum
6. Cliché des Musées Nationaux, Paris
7. Cliché des Musées Nationaux, Paris
8. Cliché des Musées Nationaux, Paris
9. The Walters Art Gallery, Baltimore
10. negativo Archivio Fotografico dei Musei Capitolini
11. Museo Nazionale, Naples
12. Museo Nazionale, Naples
13. Trustees of the British Museum, London
14. The Brooklyn Museum, New York; gift of Mr. and Mrs. Alastair B. Martin
15. Staatliche Museen Preussischer Kulturbesitz, West Berlin
16. TAP Services, Athens
17. The Beazley Archive, Ashmolean Museum, Oxford
18. Museo Nazionale, Naples
19. The Metropolitan Museum of Art, Rogers Fund, 1903. (03.14.3)
20. Soprintendenza Archeologica di Pompei
21. Hirmer Fotoarchiv, Munich
22. Ministry of Culture—Antiquity Service—KA'Ephoreia Archaeotiton
23. Sopritendenza Archeologica per il Veneto, Padova, Archivo Fotografico
24. Museo Nazionale, Naples
25. Museo Nazionale, Naples
26. Museo Nazionale, Naples
27. Soprintendenza Archeologica, Taranto
28. Cliché des Musées Nationaux, Paris

29. Soprintendenza Archeologica per la Toscana, Florence
30. Staatliche Museen zu Berlin
31. Antikenmuseum, Staatliche Museen Preussischer Kulturbesitz, West Berlin
32. Cliché des Musées Nationaux, Paris
33. The Metropolitan Museum of Art, Fletcher Fund, 1926. (26.60.89)
34. Cliché des Musées Nationaux, Paris
35. negativo Archivio Fotografico dei Musei Capitolini
36. Kunsthistorisches Museum, Vienna
37. Hirmer Fotoarchiv, Munich
38. Museo Nazionale, Naples
39. Ministry of Culture. Archaeological Institute of Dodecanese, Rhodes
40. Universita di Catania, Instituto di Archeologica
41. Trustees of the British Museum
42. negativo Archivio Fotografico dei Musei Capitolini
43. Cliché des Musées Nationaux, Paris
44. Ny Carlsberg Glyptotek, Copenhagen
45. Soprintendenza Archeologica, Taranto
46. TAP Services, Athens
47. The Metropolitan Museum of Art, The Carnarvon Collection, Gift of Edward S. Harkness, 1926. (26.7.1403)
48. The Metropolitan Museum of Art, Rogers Fund, 1923. (23.160.82)
49. The Metropolitan Museum of Art, Rogers Fund, 1917. (17.230.50)
50. Museum für Kunst und Gewerbe, Hamburg
51. Musée Alaoin, Le Bardo, Tunis
52. After P. Perdrizet, *Les terres cuites grecques d'Egypte de la Collection Fouquet*, Paris, 1921, pl. CX
53. Koppermann, Munich
54. Cliché des Musées Nationaux, Paris
55. After Bieber, *The Sculpture of the Hellenistic Age*, fig. 585
56. Kunstsammlungen, Skulpturensammlung, Dresden
57. The Metropolitan Museum of Art, Avery Fund, 1923. (23.259)
58. Cliché des Musées Nationaux, Paris
59. Cliché des Musées Nationaux, Paris
60. After P. Perdrizet, *Les terres cuites grecques d'Egypte de la Collection Fouquet*, Paris, 1921, pl. CVII
61. The Allard Pierson Museum, Amsterdam
62. Hirmer Fotoarchiv, Munich
63. Courtesy of the Museum of Fine Arts, Boston
64. Trustees of the British Museum, London
65. Hirmer Fotoarchiv, Munich
66. Staatliche Museen zu Berlin
67. Staatliche Museen zu Berlin
68. After Arvanitopoulos, *Graptai Stelai Demetriados-Pagason*, pl. 2
69. The Metropolitan Museum of Art, gift of Darius Ogden Mills, 1904. (1904.17.1)
70. Courtesy of Blanche Brown with the permission of the Graeco-Roman Museum, Alexandria
71. Courtesy of Blanche Brown with the permission of the Graeco-Roman Museum, Alexandria
72. Courtesy of Blanche Brown with the permission of the Graeco-Roman Museum, Alexandria
73. The Metropolitan Museum of Art, Fletcher Fund, 1938 (38.11.1)
74. Staatliche Museen zu Berlin
75. After Charbonneaux, Martin, and Villard, *Hellenistic Art 330–50 B.C.*, Figure 261
76. Museo Nazionale, Naples
77. Biblioteca Apostolica Vaticana, Archivo Fotografico

78. Musei Vaticani, Archivo Fotografico
79. After Charbonneaux, Martin, and Villard, *Hellenistic Art, 330–50 B.C.*, Figure 176
80. Museo Nationale, Naples
81. Museo Nationale, Naples
82. foto Soprintendenza Archeologica Lazio
83. Staatliche Museen zu Berlin
84. Staatliche Museen zu Berlin
85. Staatliche Museen zu Berlin
86. Staatliche Museen zu Berlin
87. Musei Vaticani, Archivo Fotografico
88. Staatliche Museen zu Berlin
89. The Metropolitan Museum of Art, Rogers Fund, 1913 (13.227.9)
90. The Metropolitan Museum of Art, Fletcher Fund, 1936 (36.11.12)
91. Musei Vaticani, Archivo Fotografico
92. The Beazley Archive, Ashmolean Museum, Oxford
93. The Beazley Archive, Ashmolean Museum, Oxford
94. After Hoffman and Davidson, *Greek Gold: Jewelry from the Age of Alexander*, fig. 51
95. Antikenmuseum, Staatliche Museen Preussischer Kulturbesitz, West Berlin
96. Staatliche Antikensammlung und Glyptothek, Munich
97a. Hirmer Fotoarchiv, Munich
97b. Soprintendenza Archeologica di Roma
98. Museum of Fine Arts, Boston
99. Cliché des Musées Nationaux, Paris
100. Museum of Art, Rhode Island School of Design, Museum Appropriation
101. Museum für Kunst und Gewerbe, Hamburg
102. Antikenmuseum, Staatliche Museen Preussischer Kulturbesitz, West Berlin
103. Antikenmuseum, Staatliche Museen Preussischer Kulturbesitz, West Berlin
104. Biblioteca Apostolica Vaticana, Archivo Fotografico
105. Deutsches Archaologisches Institut, Athens
106. Soprintendenza Archeologica di Roma
107. Koppermann, Munich
108. Soprintendenza Archeologica di Roma
109. The Metropolitan Museum of Art, Rogers Fund, 1943. (43.11.4)
110. negativo Archivio Fotografico dei Musei Capitolini
111. Cliché des Musées Nationaux, Paris
112. Cliché des Musées Nationaux, Paris
113. Musei Vaticani, Archivo Fotografico
114. negativo Archivio Fotografico dei Musei Capitolini
115. Cliché des Musées Nationaux, Paris
116. Deutsches Archaologisches Institut, Athens (Akropolis 1746)
117. American School of Classical Studies at Athens: Agora Excavations
118. American School of Classical Studies at Athens: Agora Excavations
119. American School of Classical Studies at Athens: Agora Excavations
120. Trustees of the British Museum, London
121. The Metropolitan Museum of Art, Rogers Fund, 1903. (03.14.3)
122. Museum of Fine Arts, Budapest
123. Hirmer Fotoarchiv, Munich
124. Museo Nazionale, Naples
125. Museo Nazionale, Naples
126. Staatliche Museen zu Berlin
127. Staatliche Museen zu Berlin

Index

Wisconsin Studies in Classics

General Editors
Barbara Hughes Fowler and Warren G. Moon

E. A. Thompson
Romans and Barbarians: The Decline of the Western Empire

Jennifer Tolbert Roberts
Accountability in Athenian Government

H. I. Marrou
A History of Education in Antiquity

Erika Simon
Festivals of Attica: An Archaeological Commentary

G. Michael Woloch
Roman Cities: Les villes romaines by Pierre Grimal,
translated and edited by G. Michael Woloch,
together with A Descriptive Catalogue of Roman Cities by G. Michael Woloch

Warren G. Moon, *editor*
Ancient Greek Art and Iconography

Katherine Dohan Morrow
Greek Footwear and the Dating of Sculpture

John Kevin Newman
The Classical Epic Tradition

Jeanny Vorys Canby, Edith Porada, Brunilde Sismondo Ridgway, and
Tamara Stech, *editors*
Ancient Anatolia: Aspects of Change and Cultural Development

Ann Norris Michelini
Euripides and the Tragic Tradition

Wendy J. Raschke, *editor*
*The Archaeology of the Olympics: The Olympics and
Other Festivals in Antiquity*

Paul Plass
*Wit and the Writing of History: The Rhetoric of
Historiography in Imperial Rome*

Barbara Hughes Fowler
The Hellenistic Aesthetic

F. M. Clover and R. S. Humphreys, *editors*
Tradition and Innovation in Late Antiquity

Brunilde Sismondo Ridgway
Hellenistic Sculpture I: The Styles of ca. 331–200 B.C.